Hypno Games

Fun developmental challenges
and experiences

Dr Kate Beaven-Marks

Copyright © 2023 Dr Kate Beaven-Marks
Published by Dr Kate Beaven-Marks
1st edition published May 2023
Paperback ISBN: 9798367095395

The author's moral rights have been asserted. All rights reserved. No parts of this work may be reproduced or transmitted in any form, by any means, electronic or mechanical, including photocopying, recording, or by any information storage and retrieval system without the express written permission of the author, except where permitted by law.

Acknowledgements

A huge and sincere thank-you to those who took the time to read and give me feedback on the drafts of this book.

To my friends, you have my gratitude for your encouragement and support, without which, this book would never have made it to print.

To everyone within the hypnosis and hypnotherapy world, I appreciate you for what you contribute to the profession I love.

About Dr Kate

For Dr Kate Beaven-Marks, the science and reality of how people are taught and how they learn, together with the impact of innovative learning strategies, have been of particular interest throughout her entire career, from her very first job teaching roller-skating (and that is another story!)

Today, Kate is a highly experienced and extensively qualified clinical hypnotist and Master Practitioner of NLP, with advanced degrees in management, psychology and education and a considerable number of hypnotherapy specialisms and advanced trainings. Kate has a Doctorate of Education, based upon the educational aspects of hypnosis from a professionalism perspective. She wanted to explore how people are taught hypnosis and hypnotherapy, and how they learn it. Sometimes there are significant differences between the two! As part of the research for her Doctorate, she completed training with many (200+) international hypnosis, hypnotherapy and related training providers and has a personal library of hypnosis-related books that would make even the most avid enthusiast rather jealous. This makes her one of the most well-rounded, highly qualified hypnotherapists and hypnotherapy trainers in the UK today.

Having worked with heavy industry, local government, healthcare services and Further and Higher Education, to name but a few sectors, from her earliest teaching roles, each has helped her widen her understanding of the influences of a diverse range of teaching and learning strategies. Keen to share her knowledge, her work as a speaker, educator and corporate trainer, both in the UK and internationally, has been extensive.

Kate is an energetic and enthusiastic trainer, with a cumulative theoretical and practical knowledge of communication, hypnosis and therapy that would be difficult to surpass. Her passion for the subject goes above and beyond anything seen with your run-of-the-mill hypnotherapy trainers. She is an exceptionally talented, honest and approachable expert in the field of hypnosis and communication.

Kate is the founding director of both 'HypnoTC: The Hypnotherapy Training Company, one of the UK's top hypnotherapy training schools, and Hypnosis-Courses.com, a leading online training provider. She has written widely on hypnotherapy, the communication, wellbeing and hypnotherapy and has been published and featured in a number of leading magazines, journals and newspapers, including Men's Health, the Daily Mail and the Sunday Times. In addition, she has published books on the topics of hypnotherapy, performance and communication. More information about these publications can be found towards the end of this book.

Table of Contents

Acknowledgements iii

About Dr Kate iv

1: Introduction 1

2: Play Concepts and Benefits 6

3: Game Design Factors 10

4: Hypno Games Structure 16

5: Preparing for 'The Hypno Games' 21

6: The Hypno Games 25

The PADLE Corporate Communications Consultancy 215

1-to-1 Presentation Skills Consultancy 217

Speaking Engagements 219

1-to-1 Presenter Coaching and Mentoring 220

Hypnosis and Hypnotherapy Training 222

Books 225

Cards 227

1: Introduction

"Humans are only fully human when they play"
Philosopher, Johann Christoph Friedrich von Schiller

This Hypno Games book provides 75 games, offering a diverse range of fun and interesting hypnosis and creative activities. These are specially designed to enable all levels to participate, from a complete newbie to a 30+ year veteran.

Engaging in these hypno games provides opportunities for teams and individuals to explore their own and others' hypnosis and hypnotherapy views, knowledge and skills.

The games can be used individually, or as a standalone organised and fun event. Generally, the games within the book will be referred to as 'hypno games'. However, the use of the games within a defined game-focused event is referred to as 'The Hypno Games'.

Most of the games can be played online as well as in-person, with as few as two people, through to as many as you can fit into a room at an international hypnosis conference, or other hypno event.

As well as the 75 games, which are clearly outlined and explained, this book also gives the rationale behind the games, their structure, how to adapt and create your own games, and even how to prepare your game participants. You may start 'The Hypno Games' as strangers, and end as friends.

This book is an ideal resource for hypnosis and hypnotherapy trainers, event organisers and any hypnotist or hypnotherapist who would like to develop their knowledge and skills, whilst having fun!

A quick note on the use of the terms, 'hypnotist' and 'hypnotherapist'. It is recognised that in some states or countries the professional title is hypnotist, and in others it is hypnotherapist. Both are referred to within this book. Many of the games within this book can easily be played by students and those who have learned to hypnotise, as well as those who know hypnotherapy.

In a hurry to get started? Then skip ahead to Chapter 6: Preparing for 'The Hypno Games' to find out the essentials, before you start using the hypno games in this book. Like to find out more about the theory behind the games? Then read on.

This book is focused on helping participants explore their understanding of hypnosis and hypnotherapy, and develop by engaging with, and exploring their knowledge and skills.

You may already have discovered for yourself that we don't always know what we know, or can do, until we have the right opportunity to find out. One route to finding out is to use quizzes, tests, formal assessments and exams, all of which have their own advantages and benefits, particularly as formal measurements of knowledge.

Yet, for many adults, tests and exams can generate worry or concern, particularly if someone has had a less than ideal school experience. Unhelpful perceptions can trigger a fight-flight response, with a resultant negative impact on the ability to access and employ knowledge and skills, particularly those that are not focused on immediate survival. Furthermore, it is more difficult to gain knowledge and build skills in a fight-flight state. Even more unhelpful perhaps, any knowledge this is gained may become connected (anchored) to a stress state.

Contrastingly, when people play, as long as the games are suitable for them and appropriately presented, instead of experiencing dread, people tend to relax. The advantage being that they are then able to not only engage with what they know and can do, they are also able to gain knowledge and develop their skills. Furthermore, when participants engage in a broad range of games, they are able to connect the knowledge retrieved to different contexts.

To optimise learning and development outcomes, we can blend the advantages of formal education perspectives, with the concepts of game-based learning and game-based development; both of which have clearly defined and highly-beneficial outcomes.

With game-based learning the focus is on the participant being better able to retain and apply knowledge or skills in varied contexts. This is particularly helpful for hypnotists and hypnotherapists who will likely work with in a diverse range of contexts and settings.

Game-based development can then be considered to be an extension of game-based learning. With game-based development, the focus is on enabling participants to access and build on existing knowledge and skills, developing greater understanding and awareness, thus increasing their flexibility of approach and enhancing their ability to be creative and innovative. This is also of immense value to hypnotists and hypnotherapists, for whom greater flexibility enables them to work more effectively with each client's individual needs and goals.

Relating theory to practice is an important aspect of many forms of therapy training and is particularly relevant for hypnotists and hypnotherapists. With these Hypno Games, participants are able to bring together ways of knowing, doing, being and responding. They can take risks where real-time consequences are limited, and where real-world experimental application may not be appropriate.

Real-world challenges and situations can often be more palatable to explore when contained within a game, allowing for exploration within interactive experiences. Participants can consider options, decide upon actions and experience consequences within the physical and psychological safety of well-designed games.

Hypnotherapy, as a profession, tends to offer few day-to-day opportunities for collaborative work. However, within 'The Hypno Games', there are a diverse range of activities for participants to work together towards common goals. This can help participants feel part of a community, rather than an isolated independent worker. Simply by playing, participants will be learning and developing without noticing, with both cognitive and emotional development occurring in a social context.

The choice of games will influence the intended development. Each game gives an indication of the knowledge and skill development categories, yet the learning will be broader, depending on what each individual brings to the event, in terms of where they are at and what they want from the event. Some of the broader areas of development include,

Attitude towards challenge
- Adaptation
- Adapting to the unforeseen
- Calculated risk-taking
- Coping with being challenged
- Creativity
- Problem solving

Cognitive and analytical skills
- Analytical and critical reasoning
- Boosting memory
- Deductive reasoning
- Logic
- Observation
- Spatial cognition
- Story-telling
- Systematic search
- Visual and spatial skills
- Visual memory

Collaboration
- Collaborative working
- Cultural awareness
- Interaction
- Peer / team work
- Role-playing
- Sharing
- Social interaction
- Sportsmanship
- Trust

Emotional
- Enjoyment
- Motivation
- Passionate engagement

Self-esteem
- Ego strengthening
- Self-efficacy

Physical
- Fine motor skills

2: Play Concepts and Benefits

Handling misconceptions and reframing play

The moment you mention the word 'play', in the same sentence as 'hypnosis', or 'hypnotherapy', is the moment you may become aware of some interesting misconceptions, such as,

- Hypnosis + play = street or stage hypnosis
- Hypnotherapy + play = disrespect
- Hypno play = messing around
- Hypnotherapy should only be serious

Rather than being a book about playing therapeutic games with clients, which would be a whole different book, this book is about using play, as hypno games, to help students, hypnotists and hypnotherapists better understand what they know and can do, whilst also helping them to develop their knowledge and skills in a unique way.

The aim of these hypno games is to help participants access, engage and experiment with their existing knowledge and skills in a safe environment, as well as being somewhere they can try new things, expanding boundaries and comfort zones. Participation in hypno games engages the imagination, and boosts flexibility and improvision skills.

The hypno games activities have been strategically designed and t in play in multiple ways, including allowing for free play to move up structured play, and for structured play to be released into free play.

Rather than being a step down in terms of conduct and standards, it can be considered that engaging in these hypno games is an activity which fuels growth and development. Play in this way can generate new insights, break-throughs and paradigm shifts. If you still have any doubts, try it!

Setting the context for the use of hypno games is important in order to create a safe environment, where participants feel able to contribute without feeling awkward or embarrassed. This is covered more in Chapter 5, particularly in the discussion about the initial briefing. By delivering a well-considered briefing to participants, you can set the tone for the events and how people will engage and participate.

Benefits of play with hypno games

In addition to direct hypnosis and hypnotherapy knowledge and skills, there are general setting-specific benefits for those participating in hypno games.

Stress alleviation

Whether it is a classroom setting and the pressure of learning, or at a conference or other public event, with the stress of a new situation, the fun of play can generate the release of endorphins, which are natural feel-good chemicals, giving a sense of wellbeing.

Mental stimulation and boosting brain function

The games will enable participants to engage with their knowledge and skills in different ways. This can promote new ways of thinking and enhance self-confidence.

...ancing creativity

...ose actively playing with hypno games will be using their imagination ...different ways. This stimulation can boost creative thinking, increase ...se of problem-solving strategies, and generate innovation.

Enabling easier interpersonal connections

Play can also cross barriers that other forms of interpersonal engagement may not permit. By collaborating in activities, sharing successes and overcoming challenges together, people can make connections far more easily. Certainly, at conferences, and other similar events, people may not chat, yet in the games, communication will arise naturally.

Personal development

Both verbal and non-verbal communication, and social skills, can be effectively enhanced during play activities. Adults can refine their observation skills (e.g., by recognising and understanding body language and micro expressions), their communication skills (e.g., persuasive and positive language), their personal boundaries (e.g., being comfortable with others in challenging and curious different situations), as well as boosting skills such as collaborative cooperation and working effectively in different roles within a team.

Play can also generate a less rigid and more flexible mindset, and boost trust, compassion and empathy, helping participants to more easily engage with strangers. This then has benefits socially (e.g., interacting with strangers, making friends), as well as in business settings (e.g., forming new business alliances and relationships).

Team roles

If personalities are known prior to the games, it can be helpful to form groups with mixed abilities and types. In addition, you may notice different team roles emerge, including,

Taskers
These people tend to look at the task as a whole and assign components to ensure the whole task is achieved. They tend to be good at identifying individual strengths and how to use those harmoniously within a team.

Thinkers
These team members are more connected to their cognitive skills and personal resources, and are great at strategy and planning. Some thinkers are more concrete and factual in their approach, others are more abstract and creative. Both approaches are helpful in idea generation and problem-solving.

Doers
These participants are the ones who put the thinker's strategy and plans into action. This works well when there is clear direction so that they can effectively implement workable strategies.

Facilitators
These individuals will bring different team members together. They will distribute resources, keep a team motivated and tend to be good time-keepers and rule observers.

3: Game Design Factors

Knowledge-based quizzes

As an individual activity, knowledge-based quizzes are useful when aiming to motivate revision of existing knowledge. With quizzes for pairs or more, by getting participants to work together you can better deal with groups of mixed abilities, and also each person will learn from the knowledge of others. Generally, quizzes work best when they are simple and fun, rather than serious and like a test or exam. Even better if there is instant or quick positive feedback or benefits. Overall, quizzes are a great way of helping participants engage with their knowledge and also to learn from the wisdom and perspectives of others.

Discussion groups

Where there are sufficient participant numbers to form small groups, such as 3 to 6 people, you can assign a topic and duration for the discussion. To get the most out of the experience, it is important to set clear instructions and ensure it is structured so that each participant can contribute. Good planning and organisation can avoid pitfalls such as not allocating the right amount of time for an activity. For example, a simple discussion will need at least 5 minutes, a complex one will need more time. With this type of activity, you can organise the discussion to,

- Generate questions for participants to consider.
- Solve problems, such as ethical dilemmas or marketing challenges.
- Find a range of perspectives on a situation, such as reframes.
- Generate a range of approaches, such as a range of methods which could be employed to address X symptom.

Debates

A more structured type of discussion is a debate. This is a great way to explore alternative perspectives for a position statement. In a debate there needs to be at least a group of three or more, with assigned roles of 'chair', 'pro' (for the argument or position) and 'con' (against the argument or position). For hypno games, choose fun or bizarre topics.

Demonstrations

Within a group, demonstrations enable participants to experience being 'in the limelight'. They get the opportunity to create and deliver content and then receive feedback. Clear parameters and safety awareness helps in the organisation of demo's to motivate engagement.

Role play

The term 'role play' when used in workplace team-building and training events can strike fear into the hearts of anyone, even aspiring actors and those fond of amateur dramatics. However, role play can be used to add a fun component to hypno-game discussions and activities. It is a useful form of learner-centred active learning which can help develop participants' abilities in exploration and draw on their own knowledge and experiences, whilst also observing and learning from others. Role-play style games enable participants to move from a passive, observational role, into an active role with stimulation combining with a sense of play and engagement in the game. There are also many types of role-play that can be incorporated into hypno games, such as miming and theatre /drama, so you have plenty to choose from.

Problem-solving activities

Problem-solving activities are great at encouraging lateral and solution-focused thinking. Examples include puzzles, practical tasks and a problem scenarios.

Case studies

In training environments, you may choose serious real-life examples to engage students and explore how to apply their learning. However, with hypno games, whilst you could make these serious, it can be more effective to make them curious or bizarre. Participants will still be able to apply their knowledge. However, it will also help them think laterally when faced with unconventional situations.

Initial 'icebreaker' activities

It is often a good idea to start with games that are fun and easy for your participants to engage in. These can help people relax into the event, start to build relationships and set the tone for subsequent games. Other benefits include,

Breaking static

Icebreakers get people up and engaged, rather than sitting, watching and letting others go first. People warm-up into an event at different speeds. Some will dive straight in to an activity, others take a while to settle in. If you started with the games straight away, the more hesitant ones will not have had time to warm up. You may find that participants who are actively engaged at the start of the event are much more likely to remain engaged during the event. Hence a great reason to get everyone doing something easy to start with. Use enough icebreakers to leave people wanting more, but not so outside of people's comfort zone that they get put off.

Developing a sense of a collaborative community

Icebreakers can help participants become accustomed to jumping straight into an activity and working together even if they don't know people, or know them well. As participants are working together to achieve a goal, it makes communication easier. Furthermore, with a well-designed activity, participants get an opportunity to think differently themselves and observe that others also may have different perspectives.

Post-event networking
Depending of the setting where these activities will be employed, participants may be creating initial connections with people they may not yet know; this can be helpful for networking after the event.

Designing your own activities
When adapting the games in this book, or creating your own games, there are some key considerations you may wish to bear in mind.

Relevant
Firstly, the activity needs to be relevant to both the event where you are using the games and to the general participant group. For example, you are likely to use different activities in a hypnotherapy training session, with classmates who know each other well, to a supervision group, where some may know each other a little, to a conference, where participants may not know each other at all.

Congruent
The activity also needs to complement the subsequent games that you have prepared. If you have a small group and have selected mainly pair work, then having groups of 6-8 participants for an ice-breaker isn't as helpful.

Transparency
It is at this point you may also wish to consider how transparent you are going to be in what you tell participants during the activity briefing. Are you going to share your rationale for the activity and its benefits, in glorious detail? Or will you let them find out for themselves.

Whilst telling people what an activity will do for them can be helpful in directing their actions, if you and they don't get the outcome you anticipated, they can lose faith in subsequent activities 'working'.

Conversely, some people prefer lots of direction and will be unhappy with being asked to be spontaneous, to explore and 'let whatever happens, to happen'.

Engagement factors

Several factors can affect how participants can engage with icebreaker activities and then subsequent games. Get it right, and it eases them into being able to engage to the best of their ability. Get it wrong, and it can lead to people shutting down, withdrawing, or internalising their discomfort.

Icebreakers have a chequered reputation. Simply mention them and some people can cringe, thinking of past humiliations from poorly designed activities in corporate or social settings, yet they can be a great way to get participants to work together, regardless of age, knowledge, skill level, or culture.

A well-designed icebreaker will avoid putting people on the spot. Certainly, do steer away from creating an overly competitive situation. Instead, a carefully designed and managed activity can encourage shy people to engage, motivate cautious people to experiment, and enable outgoing people to boost collaboration skills.

Just as we may avoid using the term 'suggestibility test' with clients (e.g., to avoid the perception of a pass/fail test), it can be helpful to use a different term for icebreaker activities. In fact, you may use very similar terms to those you use instead of 'suggestibility tests', such as 'warm-up activity', 'imagination exercise' and 'interactive energy engager'.

You will find that participants tend to engage better when they choose to join in, rather than have to. Indeed, it is much better to use a carrot here, and it be perceived as having benefits to join in, rather than using the stick, perhaps getting people to participate because they don't want to look the odd one out. Ideally, you will want everyone to willingly take part, so making the icebreaking activities appear low stress and appealing to different personality types will be more beneficial. Furthermore, by making the activity attractive to different learning/engagement styles and personality types, you will get better engagement.

Whether icebreakers or games, some people prefer to learn and engage with activities by sitting back, listening and watching first (see it then do it). Others like to get stuck in and work it out for themselves. Having a mix of these types in a group is really helpful, as it can provide balance.

Also a factor is whether someone is introvert or extrovert, and again, a balance can be helpful. If possible, avoid having one very strong individual in a group otherwise consisting of quiet or passive participants. They may back off and simply follow instructions, rather than allowing themselves to fully take part.

Another personality factor that may be of influence is that of Locus of Control (LOC). Whilst, it is to be hoped, many participants will have a relatively balanced LOC, some participants may be more towards an external LOC, with a general mindset that they are at the whim of fate, and have little direct influence of their experience. These participants can take less ownership over the outcome of any activity. In contrast, some participants will be more towards the more internal extent of the LOC scale. These might worry about the activity and 'getting it right', and may, as a result, find the activity more stressful.

Finally, another key engagement factor is past experiences; whether participants have had good, bad, or no past experiences of engagement in icebreaking or game activities, in corporate settings, childhood parties or other work or social events.

4: Hypno Games Structure

Types of games

There are two types of games within this book; 'within group' (games #1 to #70) and 'all participants' (games #71 to #75).

The 'within group' games involve dividing all of the available participants into groups and each group is assigned one or more different games. Many of the 'within group' games can be adapted to suit 'all participants', which is helpful if you have just a small gathering of people.

The 'all participants' games are specifically designed to be used with the entire participant set. The format for the 'all participant' games is almost identical to the 'within group' games. The key difference being rather than an activity card, there are briefing sheets.

Both types of games are laid out using a standardised format. This enables you to quickly and clearly decide which games are most suited to the participants you are working with.

Categories of games

All games within this book fit within one or more categories. These are,

Action

These games have physical challenges to overcome.

Action-adventure
These games have quests or obstacles along a journey.

Adventure
These games have a story, with puzzles to solves to progress the story.

Cognitive challenge
These games have tests of participants knowledge e.g., crossword, matching correct words, phrases or pictures, or word associations.

Comfort-zone expansion
These games encourage participants to engage in a manner outside of what is normal for that activity.

Communication
These games are about using and understanding verbal, sub-verbal and/or non-verbal communication.

Creation
These games require participants to collaboratively create something new, with or without props or resources.

Debate
These games explore alternative perspectives.

Dilemma
These games explore possible actions or approaches e.g., ethical dilemmas.

Duel
These games involve two people, applying individual strategy to win.

Fantasy
These games have a scenario outside of normal experience.

Memory challenge
These games have flashcard or item memory tasks.

Observation
These games involving using and enhancing linguistic (e.g., what is and isn't said and how it is said) and visual observation skills (e.g., micro expressions, body language).

Puzzle
These games are about solving a problem using logic or knowledge, or visualising concepts in an abstract way.

Quiz
The games involve engaging with existing knowledge e.g., trivia, multiple choice, or 20 questions to guess what something is.

Role play
These games involve taking on a persona.

Sharing
These games are about distributing knowledge or skills e.g., tips, demo.

Skill development
These games take existing skills and use them in a different way.

Simulation
These games emulate a real situation or event.

Story-telling
These games are about creating a story or metaphor with a meaning.

Sport
These games have opposing players, the use of dice or board games.

Strategy
These games involve using skills and tactics to achieve a goal.

Time challenges
These games are about achieving a goal against the clock.

The game format
Each of the games is presented in a standard format.

Number and name
Each game has a separate number and a descriptive name. The 'within group' games are listed alphabetically, from #1 to #70. The 'all participants' games are also listed alphabetically from #71 to #75.

Category
The game will meet one or more game categories (already mentioned).

Classification
The information in the classification section indicates whether the game is for individuals, pairs, trios, teams or the whole group. In addition, it indicates whether the activity is a talking activity or a hypnosis one. Also, whilst all games are suitable for in-person use, some games can also be adapted for online use and this will also be shown in this section.

Overview
The overview gives a very brief summary of the focus of the game.

The game
In this section, there is a detailed explanation of how the participants will engage within the game.

Online adaptations
Where a game can be used online, the suggested adaptations are detailed in this section.

Development outcome
This section gives information relating to the knowledge and skills development anticipated as a result of game participation.

Preparation, resources and props
Where the games organiser will need to prepare a location, resources or equipment, it is indicated in this section. In addition, where relevant, examples of task wording has been given.

The activity card
Generally, one activity card is to be given to the group the game has been assigned to. It will contain the following information:

Activity
- The name of the activity.

Type of activity
- The number of people in the task (e.g., individual, pairs, trios) and whether it is a talking or hypnosis activity.
- It will also show brief information about what the focus of the task.

What to do
- In this section there will b detailed instructions. These are worded in a way that is suitable for it to be read out loud to the group as briefing information.

Resources
- This section indications whether the group will need to be provided with any resources before they can start their game.

5: Preparing for 'The Hypno Games'

If you are teaching a hypnotherapy class, or are at an event and you suddenly choose to use one or more of the hypno games in this book, it is totally possible to be spontaneous. You might already have generally prepared and have had some activity cards pre-written. Alternatively, you may simply just write the key information onto a scrap of paper! It is even easier to be spontaneous in your use of hypno games online, simply post the task in the group chat.

For all events, and in particular for larger events, perhaps with multiple games or groups, thorough preparation will help everything run more smoothly. Factors you might wish to consider include assessing and preparing the location, as well as briefing the participants.

In-person or online

All of the games in this book are designed for in-person applications. However, over $2/3^{rd}$ of the games will also easily work well online, whether with a small group of people in one online room, or, for a larger group perhaps making full use of breakout rooms (e.g., on Zoom). With a little creative thought and preparation (e.g., gathering resources or props) many of the other games can also be adapted for online use.

Location (in-person)
Pre-event safety inspection
Ideally you will be able to inspect the proposed location, such as meeting room, prior to the event. This will enable you to assess the size of the room or space, and select your games accordingly (some need more space than others). You can also risk assess for any slip, trip, fall or other potential hazards and address them as needed. You will also be able to check that there are sufficient chairs, tables and other resources for your anticipated participants.

On the day walk through
In addition, to good preparation prior to the event, on the day of 'The Hypno Games', aim to have a walk through and check that everything is as you need it.

Location staff info
Where you are on the same site as other participants (e.g., venue staff, contractors, members of the public), it is a good idea to brief those who need to know, conveying relevant safety and operational information, together with who is the lead contact on the day.

Briefing participants
Prior to commencing 'The Hypno Games', a briefing will give participants a clear understanding of how the games will proceed, and how they can engage, as well as what to do if they have any questions at any point throughout their participation in the hypno games.

An example of an initial briefing is given in this book. However, these rules will need to be tailored to suit the group and the location.

Initial briefing ('rules of engagement') topics
Welcome
It is a good start to deliver an appropriate welcome, suitable for the group. This will vary according to whether the group know each and the

context in which they know each other, together with the event the games are being used within.

What 'The Hypno Games' are about
Give an overview of,

- What the purpose of the games is, e.g., to have fun whilst developing knowledge and skills.
- How the games are structured, e.g., give overview of what is on an activity card.
- What they will do, e.g., participate to the best of their abilities.

Depending on which games you have chosen, you may wish to talk about,
- Game numbers - whether they will work as individual, pairs, trios or whole groups.
- Style of game - whether the hypno games will be involving hypnosis or talking, and also whether they are collaborative or competitive in design.

How games will be allocated
Tell participants how they will get their games. For example, whether they will have one game at a time allocated, or several games to work though in the time available.

Key safety rules
For games involving hypnosis, it is good practice to have a general rule that any hypnotised participants are re-alerted (by their respective hypnotist) prior to moving on with that or other games.

Location boundaries
Within the briefing, define the physical boundaries for the general activities and also any that would seem to involve travel beyond the immediate game environment.

Questions and disputes
You may give information to the participants about who to ask if they have any questions or are uncertain about anything in relation to the games.

Additional briefing for online games
Questions
When you are organising games online, you may also wish to include information about how participants will ask questions when they are in a breakout room.

Internet connection
It is also helpful to have some guidance about what they should do if their internet connection drops.

Safety
Where you are using games involving hypnosis, have a briefing comment for the 'client', that if their connection drops, or they no longer hear the hypnotist, they will open their eyes, fully alert in every way.

6: The Hypno Games

#1 Adaptable Pre-Talk 29

#2 Aneka's Treasure Hunt Challenge 32

#3 Ask Me Anything – Truth or Lie 36

#4 At the Races 39

#5 Balloon Creator 42

#6 Balloon Hypnosis for Pairs 44

#7 Balloon Hypnosis with Groups 46

#8 Banned Words Hypnosis 48

#9 Blindfold Go Fish 50

#10 BLS Blaster 53

#11 Confidence Tips 56

#12 Creating Confusion 58

#13 Doh Induction 61

#14 Drawing Induction 63

#15 Draw It, Guess It 65

#16 Duet Sing-Talk Induction 67

#17 Elevator Pitch Twister 69

#18 Ethical Dilemma – Santa 71

#19 Ethical Dilemma – Tooth Fairy 73

#20 Eyes Open Hypnosis 75

#21 Fabulous Fractionation 77

#22 Four Corners 79

#23 Great Group Induction 81

#24 Hypno Charades 83

#25 Hypno Chutes and Ladders 86

#26 Hypno Lucky Dip 88

#27 Hypno Scavenger Hunt 90

#28 Hypno Super Hero 92

#29 Hypno Wars 94

#30 Hypno Wordcraft 97

#31 Hypnotic Threesome 99

#32 Indirect Suggestion Ball Game 101

#33 Interesting IMR's 103

#34 Lucky 6 105

#35 Metaphor Mastery 108

#36 Mime Induction 111

#37 Pass the Parcel 113

#38 Picture the Story 116

#39 Pin the Tail on the Donkey 119

#40 Pre-Talk Debate 122

#41 Pro Bucket List 125

#42 Rapidly Getting to Know You 127

#43 Reframes 130

#44 Seeking the Unique 132

#45 Sharing Wisdom 135

#46 Show Me Something 137

#47 Similar and Opposite Linguistic Variety 140

#48 Sing a Progressive Induction 143

#49 Sing a Rapid Induction 145

#50 Signs of Success 147

#51 Slick Gadget Induction 149

#52 Social Suggestibility 152

#53 Spot the Difference 154

#54 Stick Story 159

#55 Story Time (metaphor) 162

#56 Super Hero Hypno Story 164

#57 Super Quest 166

#58 The Wrong Answers! 168

#59 Timely Conditions 170

#60 Tray Memory 172

#61 Triple Promo 175

#62 Tweet Taglines – Hypnotherapy 177

#63 Tweet Taglines – Personal Brand 179

#64 Two Truths and One Lie 181

#65 Vocab Variety – Anxiety 183

#66 Vocab Variety – Hypno 185

#67 Vocab Variety – Recreational Drugs 187

#68 Vocab Variety – Sexual Words 189

#69 Vocation Variety – Group Induction 191

#70 What Would You Do If? 193

#71 Hypno Panto 196

#72 Hypno Scavenger Hunt: Team -v- Team Version 198

#73 Magical Chairs 201

#74 Relay Race 204

#75 Totally Trivia 210

#1 Adaptable Pre-Talk

📁 Category
Comfort-zone expansion
Communication
Creation
Fantasy
Sharing
Skill development
Simulation

📖 Classification
An individual-within-group, talking activity, for in-person, or online use.

📖 Overview
Game participants adapt their pre-talk to suit an assigned client type and then deliver it to the group.

◎ The game
In this activity, focused on pre-talks ('this is what hypnosis/ hypnotherapy is'), each participant in the group is assigned a client type. Participants then take turns to deliver (to their group) a one-minute hypnosis pre-talk, tailored to suit their assigned client type.

💻 Online adaptations
The activity card can be read to the group by the facilitator. It may also be helpful to post the activity card 'what to do' information in the group chat, for participants to refer to. In addition, the information from the client type card can be messaged to the group in the chat, or individually assigned via the online chat function.

👍 Development outcome

Knowledge
Group participants connect to their own knowledge about what hypnosis/hypnotherapy is and gain greater insight into what they already know. Participants also hear each other's pre-talks and this adds to their general knowledge relating to pre-talks.

Skills
Participants use their pre-talk delivery skills whilst also developing their ability to adapt, in the moment, their pre-talk. This develops flexibility in delivery.

☑ Preparation, resources and props

Space
There needs to be sufficient space for each participant to present to the group and be seen and heard. Participants can be seated or standing.

Client type card
Print a client type card for the group.

Client type card wording
The client types to be assigned are: Twin children, tree planter, juggler, pogo stick competitor, mime/human statue, costumed stilt walker, elderly bungy/base jumper, lace hankie designer, beach sand artist/statue maker.

⏳ Activity card
One activity card is to be given to the group. It is to contain the following information:

Activity
- Adaptable pre-talk.
-

Type of activity
- This is an individual challenge, talking activity.
- You will be using your hypnosis pre-talk knowledge and skills.

What to do
- Within your group, each person is to select, or be assigned, a client type from the client type card.
- Then, you each take your turn to deliver (to the group) a 1-minute hypnosis pre-talk, tailored to suit your assigned client type.

Resources
- Client type card.

#2 Aneka's Treasure Hunt Challenge

📁 Category
Action
Action-adventure
Cognitive challenge
Puzzle
Skill development
Strategy

📖 Classification
A collaborative group talking activity, for in-person use.

🗺 Overview
Game participants use problem-solving skills to solve clues and find the prize.

◎ The game
This activity is reminiscent of a UK TV programme, 'Treasure Hunt' starring Aneka Rice, who had to follow clues to a final location and prize. In this game the group works as a team, to solve the clues and get to the prize. It is up to the organiser how many clues they use and what the final prize is. It is possible to have a number of teams, and give each a different start and end point.

👍👍 Development outcome
Knowledge
Participants gain greater insight into how they and others employ problem-solving strategies.

Skills
Participants use their skills relating to problem-solving, team work, and

communication, and gain a greater awareness of how they and others use similar skills.

☑ Preparation, resources and props

Space
You will need sufficient space for the treasure hunt, preferably beyond the immediate room being used. Access to the venue in advance would be useful (for information to personalise the clue cards). You may also need permission from the venue manager to hide clue cards.

Clue cards
Personalise the clue cards to suit the venue. Hide the clue cards around the venue (where participants will have access).

Clue examples
- I am tall when I'm young and fresh, and yet short when I'm old and I can add a pleasant odour to your hypnotherapy (= Candle)
- I am there to support you and greet every visitor, but I never say a word (= Welcome mat)
- I always go both up and down, but I never move. Yet clients may need to me find you (= Staircase)
- I can be interesting and helpful and have a spine, but you will find I have no bones (= Book)
- I don't mind if you're client is sniffy. If they have an issue, I'm here for you and them (= Tissues)
- If you think you are seeing double, instead of a hypnotic hallucination, find me to spot your doppelganger (=Mirror)
- I have a hypnotic message for you, whether that makes me half-full or half-empty (= Bottle)
- I have hands but I just can't clap, although I can be so helpful in your therapy room (Clock)
- If I wear nothing but curtains when I let the outside in, could I fit in your therapy room? (= Window)

- I will make your bones hard. Your younger clients and cool cats love me (= Milk)
- When rain is in the forecast, to avoid getting wet, don't gamble, remember me before you leave the therapy room for a safe bet (= Umbrella)
- When working with children they may like talking pots. But, when that pot called me black, I said, "look who's talking?!" Then, I made some tea (=Kettle)
- Client communication can be brief or long, and delivered in many ways. For example, whilst I may start and end with the letter "e", I may only contain one letter (= Envelope)
- Client choices are great, as is variety, such as this. You can cut me on a table, but will never eat me (= Deck of cards.)
- You can see I have lots of stars, but I'm not the sky. I'll just sit here quietly until you need me before, or after your hypnosis work (= TV)
- Whatever your career, you can run with these clues, but don't run with me! Although a rock will beat me every time (= Scissors)

⌛ Activity card

One activity card is to be given to the group. It is to contain the following information:

Activity
- Aneka's treasure hunt challenge.

Type of activity
- This is a collaborative group challenge activity.
- You will be using your problem-solving skills.

What to do
- As a group, you will be given the first clue. Further clues are hidden nearby.

- You are to solve the first clue, go to that location or object, find the next clue and solve that.
- You will work together to follow the clues to get to the final answer and receive a prize.
- For example, with the clue "I dry as I get wetter and help you freshen up for your next client" the answer is a towel. You will seek out a towel and look for the next clue.

Resources
- The first clue card.

#3 Ask Me Anything – Truth or Lie

🗁 Category
Communication
Observation
Skill development

📖 Classification
An individual-within-group, competitive, talking activity, for in-person, or online use.

🏷 Overview
Game participants engage in an activity using communication, observation and listening skills, to seek the truth from lies.

◎ The game
In this activity, each participant will take their turn in the spotlight telling the truth or lying. Within the group, one participant is selected to go first. The group ask that participant a question about their therapy practice, or other hypnotherapy-related topic. The participant decides to tell the truth or lie, and answers accordingly. The group use their listening skills and observe the participant's non-verbal communication, to work out whether the participant is being truthful or not. They can ask up to 3 additional, related questions about the statement the participant originally makes. The participant's answers must be congruent to either the truth or the lie (i.e., continue telling the truth, or continue to lie).

💻 Online adaptations
The activity card can be read to the group by the facilitator. It may also be helpful to post the activity card 'what to do' information in the group chat, for participants to refer to. The speaker can be asked to minimise the group/breakout room chat and the group can then use the chat function to discuss their views. It may also be helpful to post the 'what to

do' information in the group chat, for participants to refer to.

👍👍 Development outcome
Knowledge
Participants in the group gain a greater awareness of how they and others use their knowledge of honesty markers, both verbal and non-verbal.

Skills
This activity develops participants' communication, listening and observational skills.

☑ Preparation, resources and props
None required.

⌛ Activity card
One activity card is to be given to the group. It is to contain the following information:

Activity
- Ask me anything – truth or lie.

Type of activity
- This is an individual challenge talking activity.
- You will be using your listening, observation and communication skills.

What to do
- Within your group, each person will take their turn in the spotlight.
- As a group, you will ask that participant a question about their therapy practice, or other hypnotherapy-related topic. The participant decides to tell the truth or lie and answers accordingly.

- Group members will use their listening skills and observe the participant's non-verbal communication, to work out whether the participant is being truthful or not.
- Within the group, you can ask up to 3 additional, related questions about the statement the participant originally makes.
- The participant's answers must be congruent to either the truth or the lie (i.e., continue telling the truth, or continue to lie).

#4 At the Races

📁 Category
Action-adventure
Sharing
Skill development
Sport

📖 Classification
A pairs-within-group, competitive, talking activity, for in-person use.

🚩 Overview
Game participants form pairs in the group and then race, using hypnotic suggestions.

◎ The game
In this activity, using hypnotic language in a race, the group divides into pairs. There are two roles in each pair, one is the caller and one, the race horse. All pairs stand at the starting line and an invigilator or organiser starts the race. The caller asks for a direct or indirect suggestion on a hypnotherapy-related topic, such as pain or anxiety. The race horse has 3 seconds to start to respond. If not, they miss their turn and have to wait for the next suggestion request. If they respond appropriately, they can take one (two feet together) jump forward. Then be asked a new suggestion. The winner is the first race horse over the finish line. There can be one or more invigilators checking that the answers are appropriate suggestions.

👍👍 Development outcome
Knowledge
This game encourages the race horse participants to draw on their knowledge of direct and indirect suggestions. It also gets the callers to use their knowledge to evaluate the race horse's answers.

Skills
Participants enhance their ability to spontaneously create hypnotic suggestions.

☑ Preparation, resources and props
Space
There need to be sufficient space for a start line, race course at least 7 – 10 jump distance, and a finish line. The callers need to either stand to the side of the race horse, or behind them.

Information card (optional)
To make it easier for callers, you could give them an information card which shows the structure and/or examples of direct and indirect suggestions together with some applications, such as nail-biting, performance anxiety, sport and so forth.

⧖ Activity card
One activity card is to be given to the group. It is to contain the following information:

Activity
- At the races.

Type of activity
- This is a pairs, competitive, talking activity.
- You will be in a race, using direct and indirect suggestions.

What to do
- Within your group, establish pairs, with one participant as caller and one as 'race horse'.
- Assign one or more participants as invigilators, checking that the answers are appropriate suggestions.
- Define the start and finish lines.
- Each pair is to stand together at the start line.

- When the race is started by an invigilator or organiser, the caller asks for a direct or indirect suggestion on a hypnotherapy-related topic, such as pain or anxiety.
- The race horse participant has 3 seconds to start to respond.
- If they respond appropriately, they can take one (two feet together) jump forward. If not, they miss their turn and have to wait for the next suggestion request. Then be asked a new question.
- The winner is the first race horse over the finish line.

Resources (optional)
- An information card for the caller.

#5 Balloon Creator

📁 Category
Action
Creation
Skill development

📖 Classification
A collaborative group challenge activity, for in-person use.

🏁 Overview
Game participants create a hypnotic-themed balloon shape.

◎ The game
In this activity, the group works together, using balloons to create a balloon shape that represents something which could accompany a positive hypno message which would be put on display, or used as a talking point at a hypno event.

👍👍 Development outcome

Knowledge
This activity helps participants access their knowledge of hypnosis and hypnotherapy, together gaining greater awareness of positive hypnosis-related messages.

Skills
Participants use and enhance their creative talents and how they work together with others, using communication skills and creativity, to produce something tangible.

☑ Preparation, resources and props
Balloons and pump
A selection of modelling balloons, and a balloon pump (or several).

⌛ Activity card
One activity card is to be given to the group. It is to contain the following information:

Activity
- Balloon creator.

Type of activity
- This is a collaborative group challenge activity.
- You will be using your creativity and knowledge of hypnosis.

What to do
- As a group, work together, using balloons, to create a balloon shape that represents something which could accompany a positive hypno message which would be put on display, or used as a talking point at a hypno event.
- You can decide within your group how you function, such as having assigned roles (e.g., leader, sub-teams), or as a free-for-all.

Resources
- Modelling balloons, and balloon pump.

#6 Balloon Hypnosis for Pairs

📁 Category
Action
Creation
Skill development

📖 Classification
A pairs-within-group, hypnosis activity, for in-person or online use.

🏴 Overview
Game participants, in pairs, will hypnotise each other, with dual focus and physical co-ordination.

◎ The game
In this activity, the group divides into pairs. In each pair, with roles of hypnotist and recipient, the hypnotist is to deliver hypnosis whilst bouncing/ catching a balloon; keeping it moving at all times. If time permits, the pair will swap roles.

💻 Online adaptations
The participants will need to have access to balloons in advance. However, a soft ball, bean bag, or even a cushion could be used instead. The activity card can be read to the group by the facilitator. The group can then be assigned, in pairs (or a third as an observer) to breakout rooms. It may also be helpful to post the activity card 'what to do' information in each breakout room, for participants to refer to.

👍👍 Development outcome
Knowledge
Participants expand their knowledge of hypnotising to engage with this activity whilst having a distracting physical element to deal with.

Skills

This activity gets participants to split their focus between hypnotising and an environmental challenge. Thus, developing, or enhancing, their skill of being able to focus where there are distractions.

☑ Preparation, resources and props
Balloons
Some inflated balloons.

⌛ Activity card
One activity card is to be given to the group. It is to contain the following information:

Activity
- Balloon hypnosis for pairs.

Type of activity
- This is a pairs hypnosis activity.
- You will be using your hypnosis skills, whilst also engaging your physical co-ordination.

What to do
- Within your group, firstly establish pairs; one person is to be the hypnotist and one to be the recipient.
- The hypnotist is to deliver hypnosis whilst bouncing and catching a balloon, keeping it moving at all times.
- If time permits, the pair will swap roles.

Resources
- Each pair will need one inflated balloon.

#7 Balloon Hypnosis with Groups

📁 Category
Action
Comfort-zone expansion
Creation
Skill development

📖 Classification
An individual-within-group, hypnosis activity, for in-person, or online use.

🏳 Overview
Game participants take turns to deliver a group hypnosis session, with dual focus on a physical activity.

◎ The game
In this activity, each participant (time permitting) in the group will take a turn to deliver a group hypnosis experience, whilst bouncing a balloon; keeping it moving at all times. If the group is large, or time is limited, the group could be split into two smaller groups.

💻 Online adaptations
The participants will need to have access to balloons in advance, However, a soft ball, bean bag, or even a cushion could be used instead. The activity card can be read to the group by the facilitator. It may also be helpful to post the activity card 'what to do' information in the group chat, for participants to refer to.

👍👍 Development outcome
Knowledge
Participants expand their knowledge of what is needed for hypnotising whilst having a distracting physical element to deal with.

Skills

This activity gets participants to split their focus between hypnotising and an environmental challenge. Thus, developing or enhancing the skill of being able to focus where there are distractions. In addition, it gives participants an opportunity to work, spontaneously, using group hypnosis.

☑ Preparation, resources and props

Balloons
Some inflated balloons.

⏳ Activity card

One activity card is to be given to the group. It is to contain the following information:

Activity
- Balloon hypnosis with groups.

Type of activity
- This is an individual hypnosis activity.
- You will be using your hypnosis skills, whilst also engaging your physical co-ordination.

What to do
- Within the group, each participant (depending on time) will have a turn at delivering a group hypnosis experience to their group.
- Whilst you are using hypnosis, you will also bounce a balloon, keeping that balloon moving at all times.

Resources
- An inflated balloon.

#8 Banned Words Hypnosis

📁 Category
Cognitive challenge
Comfort-zone expansion
Skill development

📖 Classification
A pairs-within-group, hypnosis activity, for in-person, or online use.

🏳 Overview
Game participants work in pairs. The hypnotist role in the pair hypnotises the recipient, without using common words.

◎ The game
In this activity, participants will pair up and take turns being the hypnotist and recipient. The hypnotist will hypnotise without using these words: hypnosis, deeper, relax, breathe.

💻 Online adaptations
The activity card can be read to the group by the facilitator. The group can then be assigned, in pairs (or a third as an observer, or second recipient) to breakout rooms. It may also be helpful to post the 'what to do' information in the breakout rooms, for participants to refer to.

👍👍 Development outcome
Knowledge
This game encourages the participant to access their knowledge of a wider range of relevant hypnosis-related words than they may usually employ.

Skill

This activity encourages linguistic flexibility, promotes the need for linguistic variety, and helps participants think on their feet.

☑ Preparation, resources and props

No resources are needed.

⌛ Activity card

One activity card is to be given to the group. It is to contain the following information:

Activity
- Banned words hypnosis.

Type of activity
- This is a pairs hypnosis activity.
- You will be hypnotising without using common words.

What to do
- Within your group, divide into pairs. Within each pair, take turns being the hypnotist and recipient.
- The hypnotist will hypnotise without using these specific words: hypnosis, deeper, relax, breathe.

#9 Blindfold Go Fish

📁 Category
Action
Communication
Skill development
Sport
Strategy

📖 Classification
A pairs-within-group, talking activity, for in-person use.

🁢 Overview
Game participants form pairs and use their non-verbal communication skills to achieve the task of catching the fish.

◎ The game
In this activity, the group firstly divides into pairs. Within the pair, the participant assigned the role of 'fisher' will be blindfolded and silent, although they can use non-verbal communication. The other person is assigned the role of 'talker', and will be giving directions without normal directional words (left, right, up, down). The aim being for the 'fisher' to pick up a 'fish' using a rod and magnet. If time permits, the pair can then swap roles.

👍👍 Development outcome
Knowledge
The 'talker' gains experience combining aspects of their verbal and non-verbal communication skills to convey directions.

Skill
The 'fisher' has an opportunity to employ their listening skills and find other ways to communicate with the 'talker' without words.

☑ Preparation, resources and props
Rods
Prior to the game, prepare some rods (e.g., garden canes), approx. 1m to 1.5m (longer = more difficult to co-ordinate to connect to the fish). On one end of the rod, secure some string and on the end of the string affix a magnet. If you want to make it easier, attach the string to something weighty and then secure the magnet to that.

Fish
Also, create some 'fish' with simple fish shapes and a magnet attached. Check that the rod magnets will pick up the fish magnets.

Blindfolds
You will also need some blindfolds, sufficient for the expected number of pairs.

⧗ Activity card
One activity card is to be given to the group. It is to contain the following information:

Activity
- Blindfold go fish.

Type of activity
- This is a pairs challenge talking activity.
- You will be using communication and co-ordination skills.

What to do
- Within the group, form pairs, with each pair having one 'fisher' and one 'talker'.
- The 'fisher' will wear a blindfold and will be silent during the task of using a rod with a magnet to catch a fish. The fisher can use non-verbal communication.

- The 'talker' will give directions without normal directional words (left, right, up, down).
- The aim being for the 'fisher' to pick up a 'fish' using a rod and magnet.
- If time permits, the pair can then swap roles.

Resources
- One rod and one or more fish per pair.
- One blindfold per pair.

#10 BLS Blaster

📁 Category
Skill development

📖 Classification
A pairs-within-group, hypnosis activity, for in-person or online use.

🏁 Overview
Game participants form pairs for learning, and then delivering a new technique.

◎ The game
In this activity, the group are to divide into pairs. The pairs will use the information on their protocol card to learn a new technique, which they then deliver. The technique the hypnotist will teach the client is bilateral stimulation (BLS), using the butterfly tap. Here someone crosses their arms in front of them, so that their fingers and palms can tap the opposite upper arms or shoulders. They can engage in a rhythmic alternating tap, approximately one per second. Then the client is asked to find an unwanted emotion within their body, and to use BLS to move the emotion out of the body. When this has been achieved, the client is asked for a preferred emotion, and they can bring that in, using BLS. Thus, in essence: Find it > Release it > Choose it > Absorb it.

💻 Online adaptations
The activity and protocol cards can be read to the group by the facilitator. The activity card can be read to the group by the facilitator. The group can then be assigned, in pairs (or a third as an observer, or second recipient) to breakout rooms. It may also be helpful to post the activity card 'what to do' information in the group chat, for participants to refer to. It would also be helpful to then post the information from the protocol card into each breakout room, as well as reading it out initially.

👍👍 Development outcome

Knowledge
Participants will gain new knowledge of a hypnosis technique, as well as insight in the application of the technique, from both delivering and receiving it.

Skills
Participants will learn a new therapy skill and then immediately apply it. This helps participants become comfortable with the concept of 'learn then do'.

☑ Preparation, resources and props

Protocol cards
Have separate technique information cards, with the protocol bullet pointed, in sufficient numbers to give a card to each pair.

Protocol card example wording
Within your pair, you will take on the role of hypnotist or client (recipient). In this technique, the hypnotist will teach the client bilateral stimulation (BLS) using the butterfly tap.

For the butterfly tap, ask your client to cross their arms in front of them, so that their fingers and palms can tap their opposite upper arms or shoulders. Then ask them to start a rhythmic alternating tap (BLS), approximately one per second.

Now, ask your client to find an unwanted emotion within their body, and to use BLS, with the intention (thought) of releasing the emotion out of the body.

Then, when this has been achieved, ask your client for a preferred emotion, and tell them they can bring that in, using BLS.

Thus, in essence: Find it > release it > Choose it > absorb it.

When you have completed the activity, swap roles (time permitting).

⌛ Activity card

One activity card is to be given to the group. It is to contain the following information:

Activity
- BLS blaster.

Type of activity
- This is a pairs hypnosis activity.
- You will be learning and using a new hypnosis technique.

What to do
- The group is to divide into pairs.
- Each pair is to have a protocol card.
- Participants will learn the new technique and then take turns delivering and receiving it.

Resources
- Protocol cards, one per each pair in the group.

#11 Confidence Tips

📁 Category
Sharing

📖 Classification
An individual-within-group, talking activity, for in-person, or online use.

🏁 Overview
Game participants talk within the group about what they did that most developed their confidence.

◎ The game
In this activity, each person in the group talks about what they did or discovered, that helped them find, or increase, their confidence in relation to their hypno work.

💻 Online adaptations
The activity card can be read to the group by the facilitator. It may also be helpful to post the activity card 'what to do' information in the group chat, for participants to refer to.

👍 Development outcome
Knowledge
Participants gain insight as they reflect on their own knowledge and experience and that of others.

Skills
Participants boost their listening and communication skills.

☑ Preparation, resources and props
None required.

⏳ Activity card

One activity card is to be given to the group. It is to contain the following information:

Activity
- Confidence tips.

Type of activity
- This is an individual talking activity.
- You will be sharing personal tips for confidence.

What to do
- Within your group, each person in the group takes a turn to talks about what they did or discovered, that helped them find or increase their confidence in relation to their hypno work.

#12 Creating Confusion

📁 Category
Creation
Skill development

📖 Classification
A collaborative group and pairs hypnosis activity, for in-person and online use.

🏳 Overview
Game participants work as a team, collaboratively creating a confusion induction. They then form into pairs, to deliver that induction.

◎ The game
In this activity, the group firstly collaborates to create a confusion induction with at least 4 components (e.g., visual, sound, movement, speech). Then the group divides up into pairs and take turns delivering the induction to each other.

💻 Online adaptations
Firstly, the facilitator may invite the participants to get some pens and paper (or they can take electronic notes depending on their online device). The activity card can be read to the group by the facilitator. When the group has created their induction, the facilitator can then open the breakout room for the pairs to then deliver the induction to each other. It may also be helpful to post the activity card 'what to do' information in the group chat, and then in the breakout rooms, for participants to refer to.

👍👍 Development outcome
Knowledge
Participants access on their existing knowledge of induction techniques, gain new knowledge from other participants, and add to their technical knowledge with a new induction.

Skill
Participants boost their collaboration and creativity skills, and learn from the contributions of others.

☑ Preparation, resources and props
Note-taking
Pens and paper.

⌛ Activity card
One activity card is to be given to the group. It is to contain the following information:

Activity
- Creating confusion.

Type of activity
- This is a team and then pairs hypnosis activity.
- You will be collaboratively creating and then delivering a confusion induction.

What to do
- Within your group, firstly collaborate to create a confusion induction with at least 4 components (e.g., visual, sound, movement, speech).
- Then divide up into pairs and take turns delivering the induction to each other.

Resources
- Pens and paper.

#13 Doh Induction

📁 Category
Creation
Sharing
Skill development

📖 Classification
A pairs-within-group, hypnosis activity, for in-person use.

🚩 Overview
Participants form into pairs and collaboratively creating a focal point for use within a hypnotic induction, which is then used within an induction.

◎ The game
In this activity, the group firstly divides into pairs. Each pair will use modelling clay, such as playdoh to create a focal point for use in a hypnotic induction. They can then employ this focal point in a hypnotic induction, whether on each other, or for another pair.

👍 Development outcome
Knowledge
Participants explore and draw on their own understanding of hypnotic focus, and gain an insight into the thoughts of others also.

Skill
Participants engage with their creativity to form a focal point related to hypnosis.

☑ Preparation, resources and props
Modelling clay
Modelling clay, such as Playdoh.

Cleaning
Hand wipes.

⧗ Activity card
One activity card is to be given to the group. It is to contain the following information:

Activity
- Doh induction.

Type of activity
- This is a pairs hypnosis activity.
- You will be using modelling clay (e.g., playdoh) as part of a hypnosis activity.

What to do
- Each pair is to use play doh – or modelling clay – to create a focal point for use within a hypnotic induction.
- They then use this focal point in a hypnotic induction, whether on each other, or for another pair.

Resources
- Modelling clay such as playdoh.
- Hand wipes.

#14 Drawing Induction

📁 Category
Action
Comfort zone expansion
Skill development

📖 Classification
A multi-role group hypnosis activity, for in-person use.

🚩 Overview
Game participants engage in a group activity, with specific hypno-related activities for 4 participants within the group.

◎ The game
Within the group, assign tasks to 4 people. The first person draws a head on a piece of paper, then write an induction next to it and fold the paper over to cover the head. The next person draws the body (trunk) and writes a deepener next to it and then folds the paper over. The third person draws the legs and feet and writes a positive suggestion. The fourth person unfolds the paper and delivers the hypnotic induction, deepener and positive suggestion to the group participants. The delivery is in some way to reflect the types of body in the drawing. For example, a smiley face (happy tonality); a muscled body (a strong tonality).

👍👍 Development outcome

Knowledge
Participants use their own knowledge and learn from other participants' knowledge.

Skills
The participant who is hypnotising will boost their spontaneous hypnosis skills.

☑ Preparation, resources and props
Drawing
Some blank paper and pens or pencils.

⌛ Activity card
One activity card is to be given to the group. It is to contain the following information:

Activity
- Drawing induction.

Type of activity
- This is a multi-role group hypnosis activity.
- You will be using your creativity and hypnosis skills.

What to do
- Within the group, 4 people are to be selected for assigned tasks. The remaining group participants will be recipients. Three task roles are drawing and naming a technique. One task role is to deliver the techniques.
- The first person draws a head on a piece of paper, then write an induction next to it and fold the paper over to cover the head.
- The next person draws the body (trunk) and writes a deepener next to it and then folds the paper over.
- The third person draws the legs and feet and writes a positive suggestion.
- The fourth person unfolds the paper and delivers the hypnotic induction, deepener and positive suggestion to the group participants.
- For example, a smiley face (happy tonality); a muscled body (a strong tonality).

Resources
- Blank paper and pens.

#15 Draw It, Guess It

📁 Category
Cognitive challenge
Puzzle
Skill development
Time challenge

📖 Classification
An individual-within-group, talking activity, for in-person, or online use.

📕 Overview
Game participants each create a drawing to communicate a hypno term, which they then present to the group, who aim to guess what it is.

◎ The game
In this activity, each member of the group will draw a picture for a hypno term (phenomena, induction, technique, theory). A time, such as 5 minutes, is allocated for this component of the activity. Then, each person takes a turn presenting their drawing and the group aims to guess what it is.

💻 Online adaptations
Firstly, the facilitator can invite the participants to locate some blank paper and pens (or suggest this ahead of time), or use an electronic means of making notes. Then, the activity card can be read to the group by the facilitator. It may also be helpful to post the activity card 'what to do' information in the group chat, for participants to refer to.

👍👍 Development outcome
Knowledge
Participants apply their knowledge of hypno terms both in the designing

of their picture and in guessing what the drawings of their team members are.

Skills
Participants engage their creative skills to express a hypno term in pictorial form.

☑ Preparation, resources and props
Drawing materials
Some blank paper and pens.

⌛ Activity card
One activity card is to be given to the group. It is to contain the following information:

Activity
- Draw it, guess it.

Type of activity
- This is an individual challenge talking activity.
- You will be using your creativity to communicate hypno terms.

What to do
- Each team member is to draw a picture for a hypno term (phenomena, induction, technique, theory). Five minutes can be allocated to this component of the activity.
- Then, each person takes a turn presenting their drawing to the group, who aim to guess what it is.

Resources
- Some blank paper and pens.

#16 Duet Sing-Talk Induction

📁 Category
Comfort-zone expansion
Sharing
Skill development

📖 Classification
A trio-within-group, hypnosis activity, for in-person or online use.

🏳 Overview
Game participants form into trios. Two of the three participants, one talking, one singing, simultaneously hypnotise the third participant.

◎ The game
In this activity, the group is divided into trios with roles; a recipient, and two hypnotists. The two hypnotists will agree on a hypnosis induction. Then, one person sings the hypnosis induction, and, at the same time, one person speaks the induction. Where there are additional participants, they can be allocated to receive hypnosis.

💻 Online adaptations
The activity card can be read to the group by the facilitator. The facilitator will arrange the group into trios and then open the breakout rooms. The trios can then choose and deliver a hypnosis induction to each other. It may also be helpful to post the activity card 'what to do' information in the group chat and breakout rooms, for participants to refer to.

👍👍 Development outcome
Knowledge
The hypnotists will engage with their knowledge of hypnotic inductions.

Skills
The hypnotists will develop their skills in being able to focus on hypnotising in a non-standard way and with unconventional distractions.

☑ Preparation, resources and props
None required.

⧗ Activity card
One activity card is to be given to the group. It is to contain the following information:

Activity
- Duet sing-talk induction.

Type of activity
- This is a trios hypnosis activity.
- You will be engaging your hypnosis skills in a non-standard application.

What to do
- Divide the group into trios with roles; a recipient, and two hypnotists.
- The two hypnotists will agree a hypnosis induction.
- Then, one person sings the hypnosis induction, and at the same time, one person speaks the induction to the same recipient.
- Where there are additional participants, they can be allocated to receive hypnosis.

#17 Elevator Pitch Twister

📁 Category
Action
Comfort-zone expansion
Sharing
Skill development

📖 Classification
An individual-within-group, talking activity, for in-person use.

🚩 Overview
Game participants take turns to deliver their pre-talk, whilst in an unusual position.

◎ The game
In this activity individuals will deliver pre-talks whilst in an unusual position. Within the group, each person takes a turn delivering their 'what I do' elevator pitch (30 secs – 1 min) in a twister position; each hand / arm and foot / leg in a different place / position, being creative.

👍👍 Development outcome

Knowledge
Participants access their knowledge whilst in unusual positions. They also learn what other participants' elevator pitches are.

Skills
The participants gain experience in delivering their elevator pitch whilst physically in a non-standard position.

☑ Preparation, resources and props
Space
Sufficient unobstructed space to safely have hands and feet in unusual positions.

⌛ Activity card
One activity card is to be given to the group. It is to contain the following information:

Activity
- Elevator pitch twister.

Type of activity
- This is an individual talking activity.
- You will be delivering your pre-talk whilst in an unusual position.

What to do
- Within your group, each person takes turns delivering their 'what I do' elevator pitch (30 secs – 1 min) in a twister position; each hand / arm and foot/leg in a different place / position, being creative.

#18 Ethical Dilemma – Santa

📁 Category
Debate
Dilemma
Fantasy
Sharing

📖 Classification
A group talking activity, for in-person, and online use.

👍 Overview
Game participants engage in a discussion of an ethical dilemma.

◎ The game
In this activity, the group discusses an ethical dilemma and how they would deal with the following scenarios,

1. Santa wants to move Christmas to July
2. Santa wants to use an adult nappy
3. Santa wants to be a naturist

💻 Online adaptations
The activity card can be read to the group by the facilitator. It may also be helpful to post the activity card 'what to do' information in the group chat, for participants to refer to.

👍👍 Development outcome
Knowledge
Participants engage with their own ethical knowledge and explore the views and perspectives of others.

Skills
Participants engage and develop their communication and debate skills.

☑ Preparation, resources and props
None required.

⧗ Activity card
One activity card is to be given to the group. It is to contain the following information:

Activity
- Ethical dilemma - Santa

Type of activity
- This is a talking activity for the whole group.
- You will be discussing an unusual ethical dilemma.

What to do
- As a group, discuss how you would, or could, deal with the following scenarios,

    1. Santa wants to move Christmas to July
    2. Santa wants to use an adult nappy
    3. Santa wants to be a naturist

#19 Ethical Dilemma – Tooth Fairy

📁 Category
Dilemma
Fantasy
Sharing

📖 Classification
A group talking activity, for in-person and online use.

🏳 Overview
Game participants engage in a discussion of an ethical dilemma.

◎ The game
In this activity, the group discusses an ethical dilemma and how they would deal with the following scenarios,

1. The tooth fairy wants to franchise the role
2. The tooth fairy wants to have a career break
3. The tooth fairy wants teeth to be sterilised and put into a box first

💻 Online adaptations
The activity card can be read to the group by the facilitator. It may also be helpful to post the activity card 'what to do' information in the group chat, for participants to refer to.

👍👍 Development outcome
Knowledge
Participants engage with their own ethical knowledge and explore the views and perspectives of others.

Skills
Participants engage and develop their communication and debate skills.

☑ Preparation, resources and props
None.

⌛ Activity card
One activity card is to be given to the group. It is to contain the following information:

Activity
- Ethical dilemma – Tooth fairy.

Type of activity
- This is a talking activity for whole group.
- You will be discussing an unusual ethical dilemma.

What to do
- As a group, discuss how you would deal with the following scenarios,

    1. The tooth fairy wants to franchise the role
    2. The tooth fairy wants to have a career break
    3. The tooth fairy wants teeth to be sterilised and put into a box first

#20 Eyes Open Hypnosis

📁 Category
Skill development

📖 Classification
A pairs-within-group, hypnosis activity, for in-person, and online use.

🏁 Overview
Game participants form pairs, and then hypnotise each other with the recipient keeping their eyes open.

◎ The game
In this activity, the group divides into pairs. Each pair will use a non-shock induction to hypnotise, with suggestions for the 'client' to keep their eyes open throughout, whilst remaining in hypnosis. Then re-alert. If time is available, then the pairs can swap roles.

💻 Online adaptations
The activity card can be read to the group by the facilitator. The group can then be assigned, in pairs (or a third as an observer, or second recipient) to breakout rooms. It may also be helpful to post the activity card 'what to do' information in the group chat and breakout rooms, for participants to refer to.

👍👍 Development outcome
Knowledge
The hypnotist draws on their hypnotising knowledge, and also learns from others., experiencing different hypnosis reactions, both for participant and hypnotist.

Skills

The hypnotist explores engaging with their existing skills being used another way.

☑ Preparation, resources and props

None required.

⏳ Activity card

One activity card is to be given to the group. It is to contain the following information:

Activity
- Eyes open hypnosis.

Type of activity
- This is a pairs hypnosis activity.
- You will be using hypnosis in a non-standard way.

What to do
- The group is to divide into pairs.
- Then, each pair will use a non-shock induction to hypnotise, with suggestions for the 'client' to keep their eyes open throughout, whilst remaining in hypnosis.
- Then re-alert.
- If time is available, the pairs can then swap roles.

#21 Fabulous Fractionation

📁 Category
Comfort-zone expansion
Creation
Skill development

📖 Classification
A collaborative group activity, with hypnosis, for in-person and online use.

📘 Overview
Game participants create then test (use) a fractionation induction.

◎ The game
In this activity, group participants will work together to create, install, and test (use) a fractionation induction. This it to include either going lighter and deeper within the hypnosis induction, or in and out of hypnosis, multiple times. It is to include,

    1, A cue word
    2. An observable action
    3. An observable response

💻 Online adaptations
The activity card can be read to the group by the facilitator. It may also be helpful to post the activity card 'what to do' information in the group chat, for participants to refer to. If desired, the group can then be allocated to breakout rooms to test the induction. Or, it may be tested in the main room, with others in the group observing.

👍👍 Development outcome

Knowledge
Participants draw on their own knowledge of inductions and explore different ways of engaging with that knowledge.

Skills
Participants boost their collaborative working skills, as well as gaining a new hypnotic induction technique.

☑ Preparation, resources and props
None required.

⌛ Activity card
One activity card is to be given to the group. It is to contain the following information:

Activity
- Fabulous fractionation.

Type of activity
- This is a collaborative hypnosis activity for the group.
- You will be using your creativity and hypnosis skills.

What to do
- As a group, work together to create, install, and test (use) a fractionation induction.
- This it to include either going lighter and deeper within the hypnosis induction, or in and out of hypnosis, multiple times. It is to include,

    1, A cue word
    2. An observable action
    3. An observable response

=

#22 Four Corners

📁 Category
Cognitive challenge
Comfort-zone expansion
Creation
Skill development

📖 Classification
A collaborative group activity, with hypnosis, for in-person use.

📖 Overview
Game participants work together to create and deliver a group hypnosis experience.

◎ The game
In this activity, the group work collaboratively together to create a hypnosis experience that could be delivered to a group of people. The aim is to have one hypnotist at each of the four corners of a room, or designated space. The hypnosis experience, for recipients, is to have each corner hypnotist with different roles that, at times, intertwine. For example, one person starts an induction, two others come in and out, and the fourth finishes and leads into a deeper. At one or more points, all four corners are to be speaking. Once created, the experience is to be delivered to remaining group members, or to another group.

👍👍 Development outcome

Knowledge
Participants expand their knowledge on how to adapt known techniques and approaches, to be able to deliver them in other ways.

Skills
Participants boost their collaborative and creative skills, and may have an

opportunity to work as part of a hypnotic team.

☑ Preparation, resources and props
None required.

⌛ Activity card
One activity card is to be given to the group. It is to contain the following information:

Activity
- Four corners.

Type of activity
- This is a collaborative group activity, with hypnosis.
- You will be creatively using your hypnosis knowledge and skills.

What to do
- As a group, work together to create a hypnosis experience that could be delivered to a group of people.
- The aim is to have one hypnotist at each of the four corners of a room, or designated space.
- The hypnosis experience, for recipients, is to have each corner hypnotist with different roles that, at times, intertwine.
- For example, one person starts an induction, two others come in and out, and the fourth finishes and leads into a deepener.
- At one or more points, all four corners are to be speaking.
- Once created, the experience is to be delivered to remaining group members, or to another group

#23 Great Group Induction

📁 Category
Action
Creation
Comfort-zone expansion
Skill development

📖 Classification
A collaborative group activity, with hypnosis, for in-person or online use.

🃏 Overview
Game participants create a hypnosis induction, with phenomena, and then use it.

◎ The game
In this activity, group participants collaboratively create a group hypnosis induction. The induction is to include IMR movement, catalepsy, and one or more additional phenomena. Where time permits, the group can assign someone the role of hypnotist and they can deliver the induction to the group.

💻 Online adaptations
Firstly, the facilitator can invite participants to locate a pen and some paper, or make use of an electronic means of making notes. The activity card can then be read to the group by the facilitator. It may also be helpful to post the activity card 'what to do' information in the group chat, for participants to refer to.

👍👍 Development outcome
Knowledge
Participants engage with their own knowledge and learn from others how

to adapt known techniques and approaches to be able to deliver them in other ways.

Skills
Participants boost their collaborative and creative skills, and may have an opportunity to deliver the created induction.

☑ Preparation, resources and props
Note-taking
Pens and paper.

⌛ Activity card
One activity card is to be given to the group. It is to contain the following information:

Activity
- Great group induction.

Type of activity
- This is a collaborative group activity, with hypnosis.
- You will be creatively using your hypnosis knowledge and skills.

What to do
- Within your group, collaborate to create a hypnosis induction that is suitable for use with a group.
- The induction is to include IMR movement, catalepsy, and one or more additional phenomena.
- Where time permits, the group can assign someone the role of hypnotist and they can deliver the induction to the group.

Resources
- Pens and paper

#24 Hypno Charades

📁 Category
Action
Comfort-zone expansion
Skill development
Sport

📖 Classification
An individual-within-group, competitive talking activity, for in-person or online use.

🏳 Overview
Game participants take turns to deliver and guess charades with a hypno theme.

◎ The game
In this activity, group participants deliver and guess charades. Each participant has an opportunity to deliver a charade, using anything other than words to convey the title of a hypno film, book, play, or person. Depending on the group, where known, you could also expand the options to include hypnotic phenomena, inductions, deepeners, techniques and styles of delivery.

💻 Online adaptations
The activity card can be read to the group by the facilitator. It may also be helpful to post the activity card 'what to do' information in the group chat, for participants to refer to. Where appropriate, the facilitator may also post the information from the getting started card.

👍👍 Development outcome

Knowledge
Participants engage with their knowledge to find something to deliver to the group and also to employ existing knowledge to guess what others are conveying.

Skills
Participants will enhance their skills in communicating in front of others.

☑ Preparation, resources and props

Getting started card
With a novice group, you may wish to provide some titles to get the group started. For example,

Films:
Hypnotic, Mesmer, Office space, The Manchurian Candidate.

Books:
My voice will go with you, Monsters and magical sticks, Hidden depths.

People:
Milton H Erickson, Franz Anton Mesmer, James Braid, Hippolyte Bernheim.

⌛ Activity card

One activity card is to be given to the group. It is to contain the following information:

Activity
- Hypno charades.

Type of activity
- The is an individual challenge talking activity.
- You will be delivering and guessing charades.

What to do
- Within your group, each person has an opportunity to deliver a charade, using anything other than words to convey the title of a hypno film, book, play, or person.

Resources
- Getting started card.

#25 Hypno Chutes and Ladders

📁 Category
Cognitive challenge
Puzzle
Skill development
Sport

📖 Classification
An individual-within-group, competitive talking activity, for in-person use.

🏷 Overview
Game participants participate in a hypno-related chutes and ladders (snakes and ladders) board game.

◎ The game
This activity uses the traditional board game of 'Chutes and Ladders' (or 'Snakes and Ladders'). The game board has squares and there are a number of ladders and chutes (slides). When a participant lands on a ladder they get ahead in the game, where they land on a chute, they go back a number of squares. Each participant takes their turn to offer a brief hypnosis-related fact or tip. Then they roll the dice and move their token that number of places. Then the next person takes a turn. The aim is to be the first to the end of the board.

👍👍 Development outcome
Knowledge
Participants are encouraged to rapidly access their own knowledge and add to their own knowledge from the tips and facts presented by others.

Skills
Participants enhance their ability to connect to their hypnosis knowledge

in a non-standard way (whilst playing a game), thus developing cognitive flexibility.

☑ Preparation, resources and props
Board game
One chutes and ladders board, one dice, sufficient tokens for each person in group. You may wish to sanitise the board game before and after use (if being re-used).

⌛ Activity card
One activity card is to be given to the group. It is to contain the following information:

Activity
- Hypno chutes and ladders.

Type of activity
- This is an individual competitive talking activity.
- You will be using a board game and engaging with your hypnosis knowledge.

What to do
- Within your group, each participant will take their turn to offer a brief hypnosis-related fact or tip.
- Then they roll the dice and move their token that number of places on the chutes and ladders board.
- The next person then takes their turn.
- The aim is to be the first to the end of the board.
- When a participant lands on a ladder they get ahead in the game, where they land on a chute, they go back a number of squares.

Resources
- One chutes and ladders board, one dice, with sufficient tokens for each person in group.

#26 Hypno Lucky Dip

📁 Category
Comfort zone
Puzzle
Quiz
Role play
Skill development
Story-telling

📖 Classification
An individual-within-group, talking activity, for in-person use.

🏁 Overview
Game participants engage in tasks ranging from puzzle completion to role-playing.

◎ The game
In this group activity, there is a container (e.g., plastic box) given to the group, which is filled with a range of different challenges, such as puzzles, hypno quizzes, role plays and curious tasks. Each participant in the group gets to select one or more lucky dips. They then work on their selected tasks, which may involve working alone, with others, or with the entire group.

👍👍 Development outcome

Knowledge
Participants will engage with their own knowledge in different ways, or develop new knowledge, depending on their selected tasks.

Skills
Participants will use or develop skills in a variety of ways, depending on their selected tasks.

☑ Preparation, resources and props
Lucky dips
The organiser will create a number of lucky dips tasks (and can use games in this book for inspiration), according to the organiser's awareness of the group's abilities.

⧗ Activity card
One activity card is to be given to the group. It is to contain the following information:

Activity
- Hypno lucky dip.

Type of activity
- This is an individual challenge talking activity.
- You will be engaging in a range of hypnosis-related and other challenges.

What to do
- Your group will be given a container (e.g., plastic box), which is filled with a range of different challenges, such as puzzles, hypno quizzes, role plays and curious tasks.
- Each participant in the group gets to select one or more lucky dips. They then work on their selected tasks, which may involve working alone, with others, or with the entire group.

Resources
- Container with lucky dip tasks.

#27 Hypno Scavenger Hunt

📁 Category
Action-adventure
Cognitive challenge
Puzzle
Sport

📖 Classification
A collaborative group challenge activity, for in-person use.

📌 Overview
Game participants work together in a scavenger hunt.

◎ The game
In this activity, the group participants are given a list of named items, or a list of clues, relating to things to find. When participants find something, they are to note the number on the item and leave it in place. The aim is to find everything and have a full list of item numbers, which can be checked against a master sheet.

👍 Development outcome
Knowledge
Participants use their general knowledge within the activity. They add to their knowledge by observing how others respond within the game.

Skills
This is great for boosting observation and communication skills.

☑ Preparation, resources and props
Cards
Print cards with photos of hypnotic figures and hypnosis-related items

(e.g., books, leaflets). Label the cards with random numbers (e.g., A4, K3) and hide them 'in plain sight' around the venue (get venue management permission first, if relevant). Remember to collect the cards again at the end.

Found list and pens
A supply of printed 'items found' form (to note label references) and pens

Master list
Also, create a master list of items and their numbers (and locations).

⌛ Activity card
One activity card is to be given to the group. It is to contain the following information:

Activity
- Hypno scavenger hunt.

Type of activity
- This is a collaborative group challenge activity.
- You will be working together to find items.

What to do
- As a group, you will be given a list of named items, or a list of clues, relating to things to find.
- When you find something, make a note of the item reference number on the card, and leave it in place.
- The aim is to find everything and have a full list of item numbers, which is then checked against a master sheet.

Resources
- The list of items to find, or clues.
- 'Items found' form.
- Pens (to note item references).

#28 Hypno Super Hero

📁 Category
Creation
Fantasy
Skill development

📖 Classification
A collaborative group talking activity, for in-person and online use.

🪧 Overview
Game participants create a hypno super hero and hero-related story.

◎ The game
In this activity, the group collaborate to create a hypno superhero, with a back story and a tale of a successful outcome where the super hero stepped in to save the client.

💻 Online adaptations
Firstly, the facilitator can invite participants to locate a pen and paper (or suggest this ahead of time), or use an electronic means of making notes. The activity card can be read to the group by the facilitator. It may also be helpful to post the activity card 'what to do' information in the group chat, for participants to refer to.

👍👍 Development outcome
Knowledge
The participants apply their own hypnosis knowledge in a non-standard way, as well as learning from others.

Skills
This activity boosts creativity skills and aids developing hypnotic

resources. For example, using in a metaphor, or when working with children.

☑ Preparation, resources and props

Note-taking
Pens and paper.

⏳ Activity card

One activity card is to be given to the group. It is to contain the following information:

Activity
- Hypno super hero.

Type of activity
- This is a collaborative challenge talking activity for the whole group.
- You will work together to create a hypno super hero.

What to do
- Work together within your group to create a hypno superhero.
- This is to include a back story and a tale of a successful outcome where the super hero stepped in to save the client.

Resources
Pens and paper.

#29 Hypno Wars

📁 Category
Duel
Sport

📖 Classification
A pairs-within-group, competitive, hypnosis activity, for in-person or online use.

🏳 Overview
Game participants form pairs, and each person aim to win by hypnotising the other person to close their eyes first.

◎ The game
In this activity, pairs within the group, engage in duels to see who goes into hypnosis first. The aim is to win by getting the other person to close their eyes. Each person within the pair will take turns delivering hypnotic induction suggestions with the aim to achieve eye closure. For example,

Person A "Your eyes are getting tired"
Person B "You are feeling sleepy"
Person A "You are wanting to go into hypnosis"
Person B "Your eyes are feeling so heavy now, wanting to close"

The suggestions bounce back and forth until one person is unable to keep their eyes open any longer. Re-alert fully at the end of the activity.

💻 Online adaptations
The activity card can be read to the group by the facilitator and then allocated in pairs to breakout rooms. It may also be helpful to post the activity card 'what to do' information in the breakout rooms, for participants to refer to.

👍 Development outcome

Knowledge
Participants use their knowledge of hypnosis in an unconventional way.

Skills
This activity encourages participants to be creative and focus whilst being influenced by distractions or internal experience.

☑ Preparation, resources and props
None

⧖ Activity card
One activity card is to be given to the group. It is to contain the following information:

Activity
- Hypno wars.

Type of activity
- This is a pairs competitive hypnosis activity.
- You will duel to see who goes into hypnosis first.

What to do
- Within your group, divide into pairs.
- In pairs, the aim is to win by getting the other person to close their eyes.
- Each person within the pair will take turns delivering hypnotic induction suggestions with the aim to achieve eye closure.
- For example,

    Person A "Your eyes are getting tired"
    Person B "You are feeling sleepy"
    Person A "You are wanting to go into hypnosis"

Person B "Your eyes are feeling so heavy now, wanting to close"

The suggestions bounce back and forth until one person is unable to keep their eyes open any longer.

Re-alert fully at the end of the activity.

#30 Hypno Wordcraft

📁 Category
Cognitive challenge
Puzzle
Skill development
Sport
Time challenge

📖 Classification
A pairs-within-group, competitive, talking activity for in-person use.

🗺 Overview
Game participants form hypno-related words from word tiles.

◎ The game
This activity for pairs, or small teams is focused on forming hypnotic words. Group participants form into pairs or small teams (depending on group size). Then each pair or team selects 15 letter tiles from a box. They then have a set time (e.g., 5 minutes) to write as many hypno-related word or terms as they can.

👍👍 Development outcome

Knowledge
Participants connect to existing knowledge and add to that by learning from others.

Skills
Participants enhance their skill of being able to rapidly recall hypnosis words.

☑ Preparation, resources and props

Alphabet cards and box
Print alphabet letters onto card and cut the card up to give one letter per tile of card. Allow 3 sets of the alphabet per pair or team. Place these tiles into a box.

Note-taking
Each pair will need some paper and a pen.

⌛ Activity card
One activity card is to be given to the group. It is to contain the following information:

Activity
- Hypno wordcraft.

Type of activity
- This is a word-based pair or team competitive talking activity.
- You will use your hypnosis knowledge of hypnosis words and terms.

What to do
- In your group, form into pairs or small teams (depending on group size).
- Each pair or team has a box and they are to select 15 letter tiles from that box.
- The pairs then have a set time (e.g., 5 minutes) to write as many hypno-related word or terms as they can.

Resources
- One box of letter tiles, paper and pen per pair or team.

#31 Hypnotic Threesome

📁 Category
Comfort-zone expansion
Skill development

📖 Classification
A trio-within-group, hypnosis activity, for in-person or online use.

🚩 Overview
Game participants in a trio have two members simultaneously hypnotise the third.

◎ The game
In this activity, the group divides into teams of three (or more). In each group of three, one person takes the role of client, one person becomes the induction hypnotist (e.g., progressive relaxation) and one takes the role of suggestion hypnotist. Both hypnotists work at the same time with the client. Where there are more than three people in the group, the additional persons can take on client roles.

💻 Online adaptations
The activity card can be read to the group by the facilitator. The group can then be assigned, in trios (or a fourth as an observer, or second recipient) to breakout rooms. It may also be helpful to post the activity card 'what to do' information in the breakout rooms, for participants to refer to.

👍👍 Development outcome
Knowledge
Participants engage with their knowledge in a non-conventional manner, giving them additional insight.

Skills
Participants engage with and enhance their ability to focus and use skills whilst others are doing something distracting.

☑ Preparation, resources and props
None

⧗ Activity card
One activity card is to be given to the group. It is to contain the following information:

Activity
- Hypnotic threesome.

Type of activity
- This is a trios hypnosis activity.
- You will use hypnosis in a non-standard way.

What to do
- Divide the group into trios.
- In each trio, one person takes the role of client, one person becomes the induction hypnotist (e.g., progressive relaxation) and one takes the role of suggestion hypnotist.
- Both hypnotists work at the same time with the client.
- Where there are more than three people in the group, the additional persons can take on client roles.

#32 Indirect Suggestion Ball Game

📂 Category
Action
Creation
Cognitive challenge
Sport

📖 Classification
An individual-within-group, competitive talking activity, for in-person use.

📌 Overview
Game participants focus on catching and throwing a ball, whilst creating hypnosis suggestions.

◎ The game
This group activity blends a physical action with creative suggestion work. Participants are to stand in a circle and throw the ball to the first person. That person, on catching the ball, has up to 5 seconds to say an indirect suggestion for ego strengthening, and then throws the ball to someone else. If they don't speak within the 5 seconds, they drop out of the circle (after throwing the ball to someone else), until only one person is left, or the activity time-outs.

👍👍 Development outcome
Knowledge
This encourages participants to rapidly engage with their existing knowledge and also to learn from the work of others.

Skills
Participants use their hypnotic suggestion skills and learn from the skills of others.

☑ Preparation, resources and props
Ball
A big (soft) ball e.g., an inflatable beach ball

⌛ Activity card
One activity card is to be given to the group. It is to contain the following information:

Activity
- Indirect suggestion ball game.

Type of activity
- This is an individual competitive talking activity.
- You will be engaging in creative suggestion work whilst in a physical activity.

What to do
- As a group, you will stand in a circle and throw the ball from person to person.
- When a person catches the ball thrown to them, they have up to 5 seconds to say an indirect suggestion for ego strengthening, and then throw the ball to someone else.
- If the catcher doesn't speak within the 5 seconds, they drop out of the circle (after throwing the ball to someone else), until only one is left, or the activity time-outs.

Resources
- A big (soft) ball e.g., an inflatable beach ball.

#33 Interesting IMR's

📁 Category
Creation
Skill development

📖 Classification
A pairs-within-group, hypnosis activity, for in-person use.

🏁 Overview
Game participants create IMR responses and then test them.

◎ The game
This is a pairs activity, creatively working with ideo-motor responses (IMRs). Within each pair, participants work out how to install Yes/No IMR responses anywhere, except hands and then hypnotise, and test using questions. Where time permits, pairs can swap so that both participants get to hypnotise and receive.

👍👍 Development outcome

Knowledge
Participants expand their knowledge of the installation of IMRs.

Skills
This activity helps participants engage with creative adaptation of a known technique.

☑ Preparation, resources and props
None

⌛ Activity card
One activity card is to be given to the group. It is to contain the following

information:

Activity
- Interesting IMRs.

Type of activity
- This is a pairs hypnosis activity.
- You will be creatively working with IMR responses.

What to do
- The group is to divide into pairs.
- Each pair of participants are to explore how to install Yes/No IMR responses anywhere, except the hands and then hypnotise, and test using questions.
- Where time permits, pairs can swap so that both participants get to hypnotise and receive.

#34 Lucky 6

📁 Category
Communication
Sharing

📖 Classification
An individual-within-group, talking activity, for in-person or online use.

🏁 Overview
Game participants take turns to complete hypno-related tasks.

◎ The game
This activity gets group participants to complete a range of hypno-related tasks. Each person in the group takes their turn to roll a dice. The number the dice lands on determines which task they then complete (max. 1 minute).

💻 Online adaptations
Prior to the start of the game, the facilitator can ask participants to locate (or make) a dice which has the numbers 1-6 on it. At the start of the game, the activity card can then be read to the group by the facilitator. It may also be helpful to post the activity card 'what to do' information in the group chat, for participants to refer to.

👍👍 Development outcome
Knowledge
Participants access their knowledge, and gain information and insight from others.

Skills
Participants use their communication skills to effectively share

information relating to the task assigned to them.

☑ Preparation, resources and props
Dice
A standard six-sided dice.

List
A numbered list of tasks.

Tasks
1= Describe your favourite induction.
2= Talk about your best social media strategy.
3= Give a business growth tip.
4= Talk about a client success (anonymised).
5= Talk about a client challenge (anonymised).
6= Talk about the best thing you learned (e.g., YouTube, conference, course) since qualifying.

⌛ Activity card
One activity card is to be given to the group. It is to contain the following information:

Activity
- Lucky 6.

Type of activity
- This is an individual talking activity.
- You will be sharing hypnosis -related information.

What to do
- Within your group, each person is to take turns to roll a dice. The number the dice lands on determines which task they then complete (max. 1 minute).

Resources
- A dice and a numbered list of tasks.

#35 Metaphor Mastery

🗁 Category
Creation
Skill development
Story-telling

📖 Classification
A trio-within-group, talking activity, for in-person or online use.

📕 Overview
Game participants creates and delivery therapy metaphors.

◎ The game
This activity is focused on the creation of a therapy metaphor story. The group is divided into trios (or small teams). Then each trio or team will select one theme, and one word from each of the 3 sets and create a metaphorical story (a tale with a therapeutic meaning) around those words. The metaphor is then delivered to the whole group.

💻 Online adaptations
The activity card can be read to the group by the facilitator. It may also be helpful to post the activity card 'what to do' information in the group chat, for participants to refer to.

👍👍 Development outcome
Knowledge
Participants use and expand their knowledge relating to the creation and use of hypnotic metaphors. They will also learn from how others complete the activity.

Skills
This game helps develop spontaneous story-telling skills.

☑ Preparation, resources and props
Information card
Create an information card with the options that the participants will choose from.

Random allocation
If you wish to make the game more challenging, you could type or write up the options (themes, sets 1,2,3) and enable participants to either blind select their words, or be randomly allocated.

Options
Themes
Growth, change, empowerment, courage, development, confidence, goals, innovation, creativity, learning, success, transformation
Set 1
Animals, trees, seasons, nature, beach, forest, fairy tale, team effort, mountains, network, perspective, mirror / reflection
Set 2
Journey, relationship, strength, power, energy, vitality, engagement, balance, focus, time, vision, future, co-operation
Set 3
Curiosity, happiness, positivity, mindfulness, patience, optimism, limitless, stability, gratitude, trust, hope, motivation, wonder

⧖ Activity card
One activity card is to be given to the group. It is to contain the following information:

Activity
- Metaphor mastery.

Type of activity
- This is a trios collaborative talking activity.
- You will be creating a therapy metaphor story.

What to do
- Within your group, divide into trios (or small teams).
- Each trio, or team, choose from an information card and select one theme, and one word from each of the 3 sets.
- The aim then is to create a metaphor (a story with a therapeutic meaning) around those words.
- The metaphor is then delivered to the whole group.

Resources
- One Information card per trio.

#36 Mime Induction

📁 Category
Comfort-zone expansion
Creation
Sharing
Skill development

📖 Classification
A multi-role group hypnosis activity, for in-person use.

🚩 Overview
The group explore reading mimes for information and then using that information to deliver a group induction.

◎ The game
This activity, for the whole group, has participants being assigned one or more roles. The aim is to have one hypnotist and one or more mimes, and some of the group as recipients. The mime(s) convey silently to the hypnotist what to say to the group for,

- A hypnotic induction
- A hypnotic deepener
- Some ego strengthening suggestions
- An awakening

The hypnotist interprets the mime's actions and conveys the mimed hypnosis suggestions to the group.

👍👍 Development outcome
Knowledge
Participants will draw on their knowledge and find different ways to

communicate that knowledge.

Skills
This activity will boost participants' observation and thinking skills.

☑ Preparation, resources and props
None required.

⌛ Activity card
One activity card is to be given to the group. It is to contain the following information:

Activity
- Mime induction.

Type of activity
- This is a multi-role group hypnosis activity.

What to do
- This is a group activity, with each person being assigned one or more roles.
- The aim is to have one hypnotist and one or more mimes and some of the group as recipients. The mime(s) convey silently to the hypnotist what to say to the group for,

    o A hypnotic induction
    o A hypnotic deepener
    o Some ego strengthening suggestions
    o An awakening

- The hypnotist interprets the mime's actions and conveys the mimed hypnosis to the group.

#37 Pass the Parcel

📁 Category
Action-adventure
Cognitive challenge
Sport

📖 Classification
An individual-within-group, competitive talking activity, for in-person use.

📖 Overview
Game participants pass a parcel, leading to tasks which a participant then undertakes.

◎ The game
In this activity, participants will sit in a circle and pass a parcel from person to person around the circle. When the bell sounds, the person holding the parcel unwraps a layer and responds to the task inside, and then passes the parcel on again, until the bell rings again. The tasks include giving tips or insights, or conducting actions. The game stops when the innermost section is reached (ideally containing a prize).

👍👍 Development outcome
Knowledge
This activity helps participants use their knowledge, together with gaining insight from their own and others' answers.

Skills
Participants engage with a range of speaking and physical tasks which will boost their ability to connect to their skills in a non-standard manner.

☑ Preparation, resources and props
Parcel
Prepare a parcel with a hypno-related prize in the middle, and other items in the layers, e.g., a challenge, a tip, a mime task, or a challenge.

Bell or other sound device
A hand bell (or another noise-making device) and a timer.

Time sheet
A sheet of paper with random times e.g., 10 seconds, 14 seconds, 22 seconds, 8 seconds.

Examples of tasks
- Name 3 time-based hypnotic phenomena (examples: future pacing, regression, revivification, time distortion, post-hypnotic suggestions).
- Mime how you would ask a client to pay for their therapy session.
- Demonstrate a rapid suggestibility test (e.g., magnetic fingers / hands, postural sway, eye lock, hand lock, steel arm).
- Name 3 alternative terms for the awakening technique (e.g.,: dehypnotising, alerting, re-alerting, terminating trance).
- Mime how you would greet a client and invite them to sit down.

⧗ Activity card
One activity card is to be given to the group. It is to contain the following information:

Activity
- Pass the parcel.

Type of activity
- This is an individual competitive talking activity.
- You will be giving tips or insights, or completing simple tasks.

What to do
- The group is to sit in a circle and the parcel is handed to one of the participants.
- When the bell sounds, the person holding the parcel gives the parcel to the person sitting next to them, and they then give it to the person next to them. The parcel moves around the circle continuously until the bell sounds again.
- When the bell sounds, the person holding the parcel unwraps a layer and responds to the task inside. They then pass the parcel on again, until the bell rings again.
- Then, the next parcel recipient unwraps another layer and responds to the task in that layer, before passing on the parcel.
- The game stops when the innermost section is reached (ideally containing a prize).
- If an aide/ helper isn't available to take on the role of timekeeper, then the group is to allocate one before the game starts.

Resources
- The parcel, handbell, timer, timing sheet.

#38 Picture the Story

📁 Category
Dilemma
Role play
Simulation
Skill development

📖 Classification
A group talking activity for in-person or online use.

📂 Overview
Game participants discuss client scenarios which are role-played by participants.

◎ The game
This activity is a whole group discussion, which considers how to respond to fictitious client scenarios. Each person in the group takes a turn to select a scenario card and role play being that client. The group then formulate 3 options for how the client's issues could be resolved.

💻 Online adaptations
The activity card can be read to the group by the facilitator. It may also be helpful to post the activity card 'what to do' information in the group chat, for participants to refer to. In addition, the facilitator will individually message participants with the scenario card information.

👍👍 Development outcome
Knowledge
This helps participants draw on their own knowledge and also learn from the perspectives of others. In addition, by playing a role, they can get greater insight into what a client may be experiencing.

Skills
Participants boost their role-playing skills.

☑ Preparation, resources and props
Scenario cards
Print the client issue scenarios onto separate cards. Client issue (all adults) examples are,

1. Nervous, worried about having hypnotherapy. Has a phobia of bent fork tines.
2. Wants to stop smoking. Has tried and restarted 11 times. Thinks it will work with the right therapist.
3. Fear of sailing boats, and new partner ridicules them and has booked a sailing holiday in 3 months' time.
4. Car cleaner wants to become a confident public speaker.
5. Retired person has just joined a university course and concerned about memory, studying and being older than the teachers.
6. Professional hugger has recently started to be uncomfortable with people in their personal space.

⧖ Activity card
One activity card is to be given to the group. It is to contain the following information:

Activity
- Picture the story.

Type of activity
- This is a group discussion activity.
- You will be considering how to respond to fictitious client scenarios.

What to do
- Each person in the group takes a turn to select a scenario card and role play being that client. The group then formulate 3 options for how the client's issues could be resolved.

Resources
- Scenario cards for client issues.

#39 Pin the Tail on the Donkey

📁 Category
Action
Communication

📖 Classification
A trio-within-group, talking activity for in-person use.

🏳 Overview
Game participants aim to pin the tail on the donkey whilst listening to contrasting directions given by other participants.

◎ The game
In this activity, the group is divided into trios, with each person having a different role. One person will take on the role of recipient, and two will be giving directions. Of the two giving directions, one will be truthful and the other lies. The aim is for the recipient to pin the tail on the donkey, by identifying the truthful directions.

At the start of the game, the recipient is blindfolded and is handed the donkey tail to hold. They will be told to listen to the suggestions they are given, with the intention of being able to put the tail on the large drawing on a donkey nearby. The two participants giving directions stand each side of the blindfolded person. They spin that person three times and then, at the same time, give the person directions (truthful / not) towards the donkey and where the tail should be place. The recipient listens for the truth and pins the tail on the donkey.

👍👍 Development outcome
Knowledge
Participants gain insight into the impact that conflicting suggestions / voices can have on the clarity of communication. They also gain a greater

understanding of how the voice can indicate truth or lies.

Skills
Participants get experience using their verbal and sub-verbal communication skills, to assess whether a voice sounds truthful or not.

☑ Preparation, resources and props

Donkey
You will need a large drawing of a donkey (outline / line drawing A2 or A3 size) without a tail. This could be affixed to a suitable cork board. There is to be a magnet attached to the tail area of the donkey drawing. Alternatively, you could use blue tack or re-usable sticky dots, both for attaching the tail and attaching the poster to the wall.

Tail
There also needs to be a string (or other collection of strands) that represents the tail. This has a magnet at the top, so that when the two magnets are aligned, the 'tail' is to be held in place on the donkey drawing.

Blindfold
You will also need a blindfold.

⌛ Activity card
One activity card is to be given to the group. It is to contain the following information:

Activity
- Pin the tail on the donkey.

Type of activity
- This is a trio challenge talking activity.
- You will be focusing on a task, despite distractions.

What to do
- Within the group, designate three participants, with each person having a different role. One person will take on the role of recipient, and two will be giving directions. One taking the role of being truthful and one taking the role of being untruthful. The aim is for the recipient to pin the tail on the donkey, by identifying the truthful directions.
- At the start of the game, the recipient is blindfolded and is handed the donkey tail to hold. They will be told to listen to the suggestions they are given, with the intention of being able to put the tail on the large drawing on a donkey nearby.
- The two participants giving directions stand each side of the blindfolded person. They spin that person three times and then, at the same time, give the person directions (truthful / not) towards the donkey and where the tail should be place.
- The recipient listens for the truth and pins the tail on the donkey.
- The remaining group participants can observe, and then the roles can be rotated, time permitting.

Resources
- Picture of donkey, a magnetic tail and a blindfold.

#40 Pre-Talk Debate

📁 Category
Debate

📖 Classification
A two-teams-within-group, talking activity for in-person and online use.

🏷 Overview
Game participants form debate teams and discuss their views.

◎ The game
This activity involves the whole group in a debate. One person takes on the role of chairperson. Then the remaining group divides into two teams, the 'Pros' who agree with the debate statement, and the 'Cons' who disagree with the debate statement.

An example debate statement is, *"This group believes a personalised pre-talk is critical for effective hypnotherapy"*.

Each team is given 5 minutes to discuss their strategy. Then, the chairperson invites each team to come up with a comment and the other team a counter comment. Participants then engage in a debate offering points to support their perspective and using their knowledge to dispute the points raised by the opposing team. If one team cannot answer, the other team get to start another comment. The debate can be time-limited, such as 10 minutes.

💻 Online adaptations
The activity card can be read to the group by the facilitator. It may also be helpful to post the activity card 'what to do' information in the group chat, for participants to refer to. The facilitator can then allocate each team into a breakout room for five minutes before bringing them back to

the main room to commence the debate.

👍👍 Development outcome
Knowledge
Participants gain experience accessing their knowledge of hypnosis, hypnotherapy and pre-talks to support their debate perspective, as well as gaining an understanding of the perspectives of others.

Skills
Participants gain experience using their debate skills.

☑ Preparation, resources and props
None.

⧗ Activity card
One activity card is to be given to the group. It is to contain the following information:

Activity
- Pre-talk debate.

Type of activity
- This is a two-teams talking activity.
- You will be debating for or against a hypno-related statement.

What to do
- In this activity, participants engage in a debate offering points to support their perspective and using their knowledge to dispute the points raised by the opposing team. Initially team are given 5 minutes to prepare their strategy.
- Firstly, one person takes on the role of chairperson and the remaining group divide into two teams, the 'Pros' and the 'Cons'.

- The 'Pros' role is to find points to support and agree with the debate statement.
- The 'Cons' role is to find points to disagree with the debate statement.
- The debate statement* is, *"This group believes a personalised pre-talk is critical for effective hypnotherapy"*.
- The chairperson invites each team to come up with a comment and the other team a counter comment.
- Participants then engage in a debate offering points to support their perspective and using their knowledge to dispute the points raised by the opposing team.
- If one team cannot answer, the other team get to start another comment.

Replace with your own debate statement if different.

#41 Pro Bucket List

📁 Category
Sharing

📖 Classification
An individual-within-group, talking activity for in-person or online use.

📂 Overview
Game participants talk about their hypno bucket list.

◎ The game
This activity, for the whole group, is focused on discussing hypno-related bucket lists. Each participant considers and shares what is on their hypno-related bucket list; things they would like to do, learn, or achieve if money and resources were unlimited. The group offers suggestions for how the participant may achieve their goal. The consideration part can be time limited, such as for 5 minutes.

💻 Online adaptations
The activity card can be read to the group by the facilitator. It may also be helpful to post the activity card 'what to do' information in the group chat, for participants to refer to.

👍👍 Development outcome
Knowledge
Participants will gain insight into their desires and use existing knowledge to help others achieve their goals.

Skills
Participants will boost their problem-solving skills.

☑ Preparation, resources and props

None required.

⏳ Activity card

One activity card is to be given to the group. It is to contain the following information:

Activity
- Pro bucket list.

Type of activity
- An individual talking activity.
- You will be sharing information and discussing hypno-related topics.

What to do
- Within your group, take 5 minutes to consider what is on your hypno-related bucket list; things you would like to do, learn, or achieve, if money and resources were unlimited.
- Then, after the 5-minute reflection, each person takes a turn sharing one or more things on that list.
- As a group, you can offer suggestions for how that participant may achieve their goal.

#42 Rapidly Getting to Know You

📁 Category
Sharing

📖 Classification
An individual-within-group, talking activity, for in person and online use.

🚩 Overview
Game participants share hypno information elicited via questions.

◎ The game
This information-sharing activity engages the whole group. Within the group, one person takes on the question reader; they can still participate in the discussions. The question reader tells the group the first question on the question card. Each participant gets to answer question 1, and then the whole group moves on to question 2, and so forth, as available time permits.

💻 Online adaptations
The activity card can be read to the group by the facilitator. It may also be helpful to post the activity card 'what to do' information in the group chat, for participants to refer to, as well as the questions from the question card.

👍👍 Development outcome
Knowledge
Participants access and reflect on their own knowledge and gain insight into the perceptions of others.

Skills
Participants engage their communication skills.

☑ Preparation, resources and props
Question card
The questions are listed on the question card.

1. Is there such as thing as a perfect session, and why?
2. Which hypno personality (alive or dead) would you most like to meet, and why?
3. Is there a place for humour in hypno, and why?
4. Which hypno time period would you most like to live in, and why?
5. How would you describe your hypno self in 3 separate words?
6. If you went back to your first day of hypno training, what would you tell yourself, and why?
7. What can you do (hypno) today that you couldn't do a year ago?
8. What do you want to be able to do a year from now?
9. Which animal best describes your therapy style?
10. Who would you most like (hypno) to spend a day with?

⌛ Activity card
One activity card is to be given to the group. It is to contain the following information:

Activity
- Rapidly getting to know you.

Type of activity
- This is an individual talking activity.
- You will be reflecting on and using your hypnosis knowledge and skills.

What to do
- Within the group, one person is to take on the role of question reader; they can still participate in the discussions.
- The question reader tells the group the first question on the question card. Each participant gets to answer question 1, and

then the whole group moves on to question 2, and so forth, as available time permits.

Resources
- Question card

#43 Reframes

📁 Category
Creation
Sharing
Skill development

📖 Classification
A group talking activity, for in-person and online use.

🏳 Overview
Game participants engage in therapy-related discussions.

◎ The game
In this activity, the group discuss reframes (alternative perspectives) for different situations and contexts. For example,

1. Snoring
2. Anxiety about eating in public
3. Performance anxiety about water skiing
4. Confidence for pole dancing
5. Stopping nail biting

💻 Online adaptations
The activity card can be read to the group by the facilitator. It may also be helpful to post the activity card 'what to do' information in the group chat, for participants to refer to. It would also be helpful to post the reframes list information in the group chat.

👍👍 Development outcome
Knowledge
Participants engage their own knowledge of conditions and issues and

alternative ways of naming or labelling them.

Skills
Participants engage their reframing skills and gain insight on how others reframe as well.

☑ Preparation, resources and props
Reframes list
On a card, list a number of topics that reframes could be created for, such as,

1. Snoring
2. Anxiety about eating in public
3. Performance anxiety about water skiing
4. Confidence for pole dancing
5. Stopping nail biting

⧖ Activity card
One activity card is to be given to the group. It is to contain the following information:

Activity
- Reframes.

Type of activity
- This is an individual talking activity.
- You will be using your hypnosis knowledge within discussions.

What to do
- As a group, discuss reframes (alternative perspectives) for different situations and contexts, as listed on the reframes list.

Resources
- Reframes list.

#44 Seeking the Unique

📁 Category
Cognitive challenge
Puzzle
Skill development
Sport
Time challenge

📖 Classification
An individual-within-group, competitive talking activity, for in-person and online use.

⚐ Overview
Game participants use their hypno knowledge in a competitive game.

◎ The game
In this activity, there are 15 activity themes which are worked through in order. For each activity theme, participants have 2 minutes to come up with one or more words or phrases that are hypno-related. Those who do not come up with a word, miss the next round. For those who did generate words, these are compared and where others have the same word, that word is crossed off each person's list. The winner is the person at the end with the highest number of unique words.

💻 Online adaptations
Prior to commencing the game, the facilitator could invite participants to get a pen and some paper, or open an online document to make notes in. The activity card can be read to the group by the facilitator. It may also be helpful to post the activity card 'what to do' information in the group chat, for participants to refer to as well as the activity theme list. Alternatively, the facilitator can share the activity themes one at a time

to avoid participants preparing ahead.

👍👍 Development outcome
Knowledge
The participants get to access their own knowledge.

Skills
Participants will rapidly access their knowledge and use strategic thinking to consider potentially unique responses.

☑ Preparation, resources and props
Note-taking
Sufficient paper and pens for the participants in the group.

Activity theme card
The activity themes can be printed on a separate card,

1. TV programme
2. Public figure
3. Reasons to make a phone call
4. Nouns
5. Film / movie
6. Event or festival
7. Verbs
8. Job titles people may have
9. Reasons to send an email
10. Locations
11. What makes you smile
12. Equipment
13. Adjectives
14. Reasons to call the emergency services
15. Things you can buy that you need to save up for

⏳ Activity card

One activity card is to be given to the group. It is to contain the following information:

Activity
- Seeking the unique.

Type of activity
- This is an individual competitive talking activity.
- You will be using your general hypnosis knowledge within a number of themes.

What to do
- In this game, there are 15 activity themes listed, which are worked through in order.
- For each activity theme, you will have 2 minutes to come up with one or more words or phrases that is hypno-related.
- Those participants who do not come up with a word, miss the next round.
- At the end of the 15 activity themes, for those who did generate words, these are compared and where others have the same word, that word is crossed off each person's list.
- The winner is the person at the end with the highest number of unique words.

Resources
- The activity theme card, pens and paper.

#45 Sharing Wisdom

📁 Category
Sharing

📖 Classification
An individual-within-group, talking activity for in-person and online use.

🏁 Overview
Game participants share hypnosis knowledge.

◎ The game
This activity, for the whole group, is focused on sharing hypno knowledge. One person takes on the role of timekeeper. Each group member then takes a turn to spend 2 minutes sharing their top tip on a hypno topic.

💻 Online adaptations
The activity card can be read to the group by the facilitator. It may also be helpful to post the activity card 'what to do' information in the group chat, for participants to refer to.

👍👍 Development outcome

Knowledge
Participants access their own knowledge and gain insight from what they know and what others share.

Skills
Participants gain experience in presenting information to a group.

☑ Preparation, resources and props
None

⏳ Activity card

One activity card is to be given to the group. It is to contain the following information:

Activity
- Sharing wisdom.

Type of activity
- This is an individual talking activity.
- You will be sharing hypnosis-relating information.

What to do
- Within your group you will be sharing knowledge.
- One person is to take on the role of timekeeper.
- Each group member then takes a turn to spend 2 minutes sharing their top tip on a hypno topic.

#46 Show Me Something

📁 Category
Comfort-zone expansion
Creation
Sharing
Skill development

📖 Classification
A group collaboration and Individual-within-group, hypnosis activity, for in-person and online use.

🗂 Overview
Game participants collaborate to create a hypno demo concept and then take turns delivering their version of it.

◎ The game
In this activity, there is a group activity component and an individual presentation and demonstration component. Firstly, the group will collaborate to create a hypnosis demonstration concept. A theme could be assigned to this game. For example, demonstrations relating to specific hypnotic phenomena (e.g., catalepsy), or relating to certain techniques (e.g., anchoring), or how hypnotherapy can help certain issues (e.g., an anxiety-alleviation approach). Each individual can then consider how they could put their own individual perspective into the demonstration. Finally, each person will present the demonstration to the group with one different component.

💻 Online adaptations
Before the game starts, the facilitator can invite participants to locate a pen and paper (or suggest this ahead of time), or open an online note-taking function. The activity card can then be read to the group by the facilitator. It may also be helpful to post the activity card 'what to do'

information in the group chat, for participants to refer to.

👍👍 Development outcome
Knowledge
Participants draw on their knowledge to contribute to the demo concept and gain insight from the contributions of others.

Skills
Participants gain experience in presenting and demonstrating, whilst having to spontaneously change aspects of a plan.

☑ Preparation, resources and props
Note-taking
Pens and paper.

⏳ Activity card
One activity card is to be given to the group. It is to contain the following information:

Activity
- Show me something.

Type of activity
- This is both a group collaboration and individual hypnosis activity.
- You will be using your creativity, presentation and demonstration skills.

What to do
- In this activity, there is a group activity component and an individual presentation and demonstration component.
- Firstly, as a group, collaborate to create a hypnosis demonstration concept.

- Each individual then considers how they could put their own individual perspective into the demonstration.
- Finally, each person presents the demonstration to the group with one different component.

Resources
- Pens and paper.

#47 Similar and Opposite Linguistic Variety

📁 Category
Creation
Cognitive challenge
Sharing
Skill development

📖 Classification
A group discussion activity, for in-person and online use.

📕 Overview
Game participants explore their use of hypno-related words.

◎ The game
In this activity, the group will discuss similar and alternative words for hypno-related terms. This can either be until there are no new words arising, or time-based (e.g., 1-minute or 2-minutes per word). Hypno-related words can include,

- Anxiety
- Happiness
- Stress
- Phobia
- Consultation
- Confidentiality
- Ego strength
- Session fee

💻 Online adaptations
The activity card can be read to the group by the facilitator. It may also

be helpful to post the activity card 'what to do' information in the group chat, for participants to refer to, as well as the information from the hypnosis-related words card.

👍👍 Development outcome

Knowledge
Participants explore their own linguistic range and learn from others.

Skills
Participants engage and develop their discussion skills.

☑ Preparation, resources and props

Hypnosis-related words card
The hypno-related words are to be written or printed on a separate card.

Hypnosis-related word examples,
- Anxiety
- Happiness
- Stress
- Phobia
- Consultation
- Confidentiality
- Ego strength
- Session fee

⧖ Activity card
One activity card is to be given to the group. It is to contain the following information:

Activity
- Similar and opposite linguistic variety.

Type of activity
- This is a group discussion activity.

- You will be exploring similar and alternative words for hypno-related terms.

What to do
- As a group, you will discuss similar and alternative words for those listed on the hypnosis-related words card.
- The discussion can either be until there are no new words arising for a particular word or phrase, or it can be time-based (e.g., 1-minute or 2-minutes per word).

Resources
- Hypnosis-related words card.

#48 Sing a Progressive Induction

📁 Category
Comfort-zone expansion
Sharing
Skill development

📖 Classification
An individual-within-group, hypnosis activity, for in-person and online use.

🚩 Overview
Game participants take turns to sing a group hypnosis induction.

◎ The game
In this activity, within the group, one person is assigned as hypnotist, and they will sing a progressive relaxation hypnotic induction to the rest of the group. The hypnotist then re-alerts the group. Another person then takes on the hypnotist role.

💻 Online adaptations
The activity card can be read to the group by the facilitator. It may also be helpful to post the activity card 'what to do' information in the group chat, for participants to refer to.

👍👍 Development outcome
Knowledge
Participants access their knowledge of progressive relaxation inductions and gain insight into non-standard delivery.

Skills
Participants boost their group hypnosis skills, and gain confidence in

delivering a hypnotic induction in a non-standard way.

☑ Preparation, resources and props
None

⌛ Activity card
One activity card is to be given to the group. It is to contain the following information:

Activity
- Sing a progressive induction.

Type of activity
- This is an individual hypnosis activity.
- You will be using hypnosis in a non-standard way.

What to do
- Within the group, one person is assigned as hypnotist, and they will sing a progressive relaxation hypnotic induction to the rest of the group and then the hypnotist re-alerts the group.
- Another person then takes on the hypnotist role.

#49 Sing a Rapid Induction

📁 Category
Comfort-zone expansion
Sharing
Skill development

📖 Classification
A pairs-within-group, hypnosis activity, for in-person and online use.

🗺 Overview
Game participants sing a hypnosis induction to their pair partner.

◎ The game
For this activity, the group divides into pairs. One person in each pair is assigned as recipient, one as hypnotist. The hypnotist will sing rather than speak a rapid hypnosis induction. They will then re-alert their recipient and then swap roles.

💻 Online adaptations
The activity card can be read to the group by the facilitator. The group can then be assigned, in pairs (or a third as an observer, or second recipient) to breakout rooms. It may also be helpful to post the activity card 'what to do' information in the breakout rooms, for participants to refer to.

👍👍 Development outcome
Knowledge
Participants access their knowledge of rapid inductions and gain insight into non-standard delivery.

Skills
Participants boost their hypnosis skills by delivering a rapid hypnosis induction in a different way.

☑ Preparation, resources and props
None required.

⏳ Activity card
One activity card is to be given to the group. It is to contain the following information:

Activity
- Sing a rapid induction.

Type of activity
- This is a pairs hypnosis activity.
- You will be using hypnosis in a non-standard way.

What to do
- As a group divide up into pairs.
- Within each pair, one person takes the role of recipient and one as a hypnotist. The hypnotist will sing rather than speak a rapid hypnosis induction.
- They will then re-alert their recipient and swap roles.

#50 Signs of Success

📁 Category
Sharing

📖 Classification
A group talking activity, for in-person and online use.

🏁 Overview
The group discuss signs of success.

🎯 The game
This is a group discussion activity, focused on signs of success. Each participant within the group takes a turn to introduce what they consider to be a sign of success, and the group then discusses that, before moving on to the next participant's offered sign.

💻 Online adaptations
The activity card can be read to the group by the facilitator. It may also be helpful to post the activity card 'what to do' information in the group chat, for participants to refer to.

👍👍 Development outcome

Knowledge
Participants gain insight into their own perspectives of success and those of others.

Skills
Participants boost their communication skills.

☑ Preparation, resources and props
None.

⌛ Activity card

One activity card is to be given to the group. It is to contain the following information:

Activity
- Signs of success.

Type of activity
- This is a group discussion activity.
- Your discussion will be focused on signs of success.

What to do
- Within the group, each participant takes a turn to introduce what they consider to be a sign of success.
- The group then discusses that, before moving on to the next participant's offered sign of success.

#51 Slick Gadget Induction

📁 Category
Action
Creation
Comfort-zone expansion
Creation
Skill development

📖 Classification
A collaborative group activity, with hypnosis, for in-person or online use.

🗒 Overview
Game participants collaborate to create and then deliver a hypnosis induction.

◎ The game
This is a group activity, involving the creative use of a gadget as part of a hypnotic induction. Firstly, the group will collaborate and create a hypnotic induction that makes use the gadget they have selected, or been allocated. When that phase of the activity has been completed, the group nominates one person to deliver the induction, either to an individual or the group, as appropriate for the design of the induction.

💻 Online adaptations
Before the game begins, the facilitator is to ask the group members to locate a common household item, such as a pen, a fork, or some other item. The activity card can be read to the group by the facilitator and the group collaborate on creating the induction. One person then delivers that induction. It may also be helpful to post the 'what to do' information in the group chat, for participants to refer to.

👍👍 Development outcome
Knowledge
Participants use and expand their hypnosis induction knowledge and learn from the perspectives and knowledge of others.

Skills
Participants engage their creative skills and boost their confidence delivering a non-standard induction.

☑ Preparation, resources and props
Gadgets
One of more gadgets, such as a tape measure, a sand-filled egg timer, pen light, bean bag, or a childhood toy such as Rubik or puzzle cube, spinning top, magic snake, slinky or yoyo.

⏳ Activity card
One activity card is to be given to the group. It is to contain the following information:

Activity
- Slick gadget induction.

Type of activity
- This is a collaborative group hypnosis activity.
- You will be finding a way of using a gadget as part of a hypnotic induction.

What to do
- This is a group activity, involving the creative use of a gadget as part of a hypnotic induction.
- Firstly, as a group, collaborate and create a hypnotic induction that makes use the gadget you have selected, or been allocated.
- When that phase of the activity has been completed, the group nominates one person to deliver the induction, either to an

individual or the group, as appropriate for the design of the induction.

Resources
- One of more gadgets, such as a tape measure, a sand-filled egg timer, pen light, bean bag, or a childhood toy such as Rubik or puzzle cube, spinning top, magic snake, slinky or yoyo.

#52 Social Suggestibility

📁 Category
Creation
Skill development

📖 Classification
A collaborative group and pairs hypnosis activity, for in-person use.

🏳 Overview
Game participants create a movement or catalepsy suggestibility test and then use it, in pairs, in a public environment.

◎ The game
In this group and pairs activity, participants creatively use hypnotic phenomena and suggestibility. The group works together to develop a moving or sticking (movement IMR or catalepsy) suggestibility test. Then, they pair up and take turns to deliver it somewhere nearby, where other people can see them, before returning to the games room.

👍👍 Development outcome
Knowledge
Participants engage with their knowledge of hypnotic phenomena and suggestibility testing, using both to create something new, thus gaining new knowledge. In addition, participants will learn from the contributions of others within the group.

Skills
Participants engage with their creativity and develop their suggestibility testing skills by learning a new suggestibility test. They will also gain confidence working in public.

☑ Preparation, resources and props
Note-taking
Pens and paper.

⌛ Activity card
One activity card is to be given to the group. It is to contain the following information:

Activity
- Social suggestibility.

Type of activity
- This is a group and then pairs creative hypnosis activity.
- You will be using hypnotic phenomena and suggestibility.

What to do
- As a group, work together to develop a moving or sticking (movement IMR or catalepsy) suggestibility test.
- Then, pair up and deliver it somewhere nearby where other people can see you (and then come back to the games room).

Resources
- Pens and paper.

#53 Spot the Difference

📁 Category
Cognitive challenge
Puzzle
Quiz
Sport

📖 Classification
A pairs-within-group, competitive talking activity for in-person or online use.

🏳 Overview
Game participants form into pairs and spot the differences between two images.

◎ The game
The group forms pairs and have a spot the difference activity sheet, which has two images with subtle differences. Participants are to note on one image the differences. The winners are those who find all the differences first, or, if a time-challenge, who finds the greatest number of differences in the allocated time.

💻 Online adaptations
The activity card can be read to the group by the facilitator. It may also be helpful to post the activity card 'what to do' information in the group chat, for participants to refer to. The facilitator can then allocate participants in pairs to breakout rooms. The two 'differences' images can then be posted in each room. Participants can note the location of the differences. The solution photo can then be shared.

👍👍 Development outcome
Knowledge
Participants gain awareness of how others look for differences and the impact that a time challenge may or may not have.

Skills
Participants will be able to hone their communication and observation skills.

☑ Preparation, resources and props
Image sheet
A spot the difference activity sheet, which has two images with subtle differences. Also prepare a separate 'these are the answers' sheet.

⌛ Activity card
One activity card is to be given to the group. It is to contain the following information:

Activity
- Spot the difference.

Type of activity
- This is a pairs competitive talking activity.
- You will be using your observation skills.

What to do
- In the group, divide up to forms pairs.
- Each pair is to have a spot the difference activity sheet, which has two images with subtle differences.
- Participants are to note on one image the differences between the two images.
- The winners are those who find all the differences first, or, if a time-challenge, who finds the greatest number of differences in the allocated time.

Resources
- Activity sheet with the two 'differences' images.
- A separate 'these are the answers' sheet.

Image 1

Image 2

Solution

#54 Stick Story

📁 Category
Adventure
Comfort-zone expansion
Creation
Skill development
Story telling

📖 Classification
A collaborative group talking activity, for in-person use.

🚩 Overview
Game participants create a shared story.

◎ The game
In this activity, the whole group collaborate to create a story. There is a 'story stick' which is passed around the group. When a participant receives the story stick, they are to say one sentence that contributes to a story about a sport person benefitting from hypnosis. A facilitator (appointed within the group, or provided by the organiser) has 5 variant cards they can add in at any time. These variations need to be incorporated into the story within the next 5 sentences.

👍👍 Development outcome
Knowledge
Participants increase their story-telling knowledge by experiencing the actions of others within the group.

Skills
Participants develop their story-telling skills.

☑ Preparation, resources and props
The stick
Create a story-telling stick. This can be anything from a piece of cardboard to something elaboratively creative and highly decorated.

Variant cards
Print or write out the variant cards, with the words,

- A banana
- A balloon
- A frog
- An American flag
- A flat tyre

⌛ Activity card
One activity card is to be given to the group. It is to contain the following information:

Activity
- Stick story.

Type of activity
- This is a collaborative group talking activity.
- You will be using your story-telling skills.

What to do
- In this story-telling whole group activity, there is a 'story stick' which will be passed around the members of the group.
- When a participant receives the story stick, they are to say one sentence that contributes to a story about a sport person benefitting from hypnosis.
- A facilitator (appointed within the group, or provided by the organiser) has 5 variant cards they can add in at any time. These

variations need to be incorporated into the story within the next 5 sentences.

Resources
- The 'story stick'.
- The 5 variant cards.

#55 Story Time (metaphor)

📁 Category
Creation
Story-telling

📖 Classification
A collaborative group talking activity, for in-person or online use.

📲 Overview
Game participants create a hypnotic metaphor using hypnotic language phrases.

◎ The game
This group activity involves working collaboratively, using hypnotic language phrases, to dynamically create a hypnotic metaphor. The group form a circle and take turns using one hypnotic language phrase type per person, whilst creating a hypnotic metaphor story (story with a meaning).

💻 Online adaptations
The activity card can be read to the group by the facilitator. It may also be helpful to post the activity card 'what to do' information in the group chat, for participants to refer to.

👍👍 Development outcome
Knowledge
Participants draw on their existing knowledge of language patterns and metaphor formation and gain awareness of how others work.

Skills
Participants gain experience in rapidly engaging their language pattern application and metaphor creation skills, whilst collaboratively working

with others.

☑ Preparation, resources and props

Although you can work entirely resource free, it may helpful to have some crib cards showing different hypnotic language patterns, or using the pre-printed cards available from hypnosis-courses.com (Hypnotic Language Cards).

⧖ Activity card

One activity card is to be given to the group. It is to contain the following information:

Activity
- Story time (metaphor).

Type of activity
- This is a collaborative group talking activity.
- You will be using hypnotic language phrases to create a hypnotic metaphor.

What to do
- Within your group, form a circle and take turns using one hypnotic language phrase type per person, whilst creating a hypnotic metaphor story (story with a meaning).

#56 Super Hero Hypno Story

📁 Category
Action-adventure
Creation
Fantasy
Skill development
Story telling

📖 Classification
A creative collaborative group activity, for in-person and online use.

📒 Overview
Game participants create a superhero and associated story.

◎ The game
The group work together to create the concept of a hypnotic super hero. Then, they create a story about how the hero uses hypnosis to win over evil, including at least 3 obstacles.

💻 Online adaptations
Prior to the game starting, the facilitator can invite participants to locate a pen and paper (or suggest this ahead of time), or open an online note-taking resource. The activity card can then be read to the group by the facilitator. It may also be helpful to post the activity card 'what to do' information in the group chat, for participants to refer to.

👍👍 Development outcome
Knowledge
Participants engage with their broad knowledge of hypnosis, together with their general knowledge, to contribute to a group creative concept.

Skills
Participants boost their creative and collaboration skills.

☑ Preparation, resources and props
Note-taking
Pens and paper.

⌛ Activity card
One activity card is to be given to the group. It is to contain the following information:

Activity
- Super hero hypno story.

Type of activity
- This is a collaborative talking activity for the whole group.
- You will be using your creativity and knowledge of hypnosis.

What to do
- As a group, you are to work together and collaboratively create the concept of a hypnotic super hero.
- Then, create a story about how the hero uses hypnosis to win over evil, including at least 3 obstacles.

Resources
- Pens and paper.

#57 Super Quest

📁 Category
Action-adventure
Fantasy
Role playing

📖 Classification
A collaborative group talking activity, for in-person or online use.

🚩 Overview
Game participants create a story about overcoming adversity.

◎ The game
In this activity, the whole group work together to create a story about someone overcoming adversity. The group work together to create a fantasy story of a quest where the person on the quest uses hypnosis in some way to go on a journey of discovery, overcome challenges and reach their goal. Where time permits, they will present their story to another group.

💻 Online adaptations
Prior to the game starting, the facilitator can invite participants to locate a pen and paper (or request this ahead of time), or open an online note-taking resource. The activity card can then be read to the group by the facilitator. It may also be helpful to post the activity card 'what to do' information in the group chat, for participants to refer to.

👍👍 Development outcome
Knowledge
Participants use their knowledge of story-telling to contribute to the story creation. In addition, they gain awareness and insight into the story-

telling processes of others in the group.

Skills
Participants boost their creative and collaboration skills.

☑ Preparation, resources and props
Note-taking
Pens and paper.

⌛ Activity card
One activity card is to be given to the group. It is to contain the following information:

Activity
- Super quest.

Type of activity
- This is a collaborative talking activity for the whole group.
- You will be using your creativity and story-telling skills.

What to do
- This is a collaborative whole group activity. You will be creating a quest-style story about someone overcoming adversity.
- The group work together to create a fantasy-style story, where the person on the quest uses hypnosis in some way to go on a journey of discovery, overcome challenges and reach their goal.
- Where time permits, they will present their story to another group.

Resources
Pens and paper.

#58 The Wrong Answers!

📁 Category
Creation
Role play
Simulation

📖 Classification
An individual-within-group, competitive talking activity, for in-person and online use.

🏳 Overview
Game participants deliver and assess role plays relating to hypnosis interviews.

◎ The game
In this creative role-playing activity, some of the group take on roles and others are observers. Within the group, one person takes on the role of a radio interviewer and another the person being interviewed about hypno (for 2 minutes). The person being interviewed aims to give the most incorrect and bizarre answers they can. Then the roles rotate to other group members. At the end, the group decides which role-player was the most creative with their answers.

💻 Online adaptations
The activity card can be read to the group by the facilitator. It may also be helpful to post the 'what to do' information in the group chat, for participants to refer to.

👍👍 Development outcome
Knowledge
Participants access their general knowledge about hypnosis and rapidly

change fact into fiction as part of the activity.

Skill
Participants have an opportunity boost their ability to think on their feet.

☑ Preparation, resources and props
None required.

⌛ Activity card
One activity card is to be given to the group. It is to contain the following information:

Activity
- The wrong answers!

Type of activity
- This is an individual talking activity.
- You will be using your creativity and role-playing skills.

What to do
- This is a creative role-playing activity. Within the group, one person takes on the role of a radio interviewer and another the person being interviewed about hypno (for 2 minutes).
- The person being interviewed aims to give the most incorrect and bizarre answers they can.
- Then the roles rotate to other group members.
- At the end, the group decides which role-player was the most creative with their answers.

#59 Timely Conditions

📁 Category
Action
Comfort-zone expansion
Sport
Time challenge

📖 Classification
An individual-within-group activity, for in-person and online use.

🏳 Overview
Game participants watch, deliver and assess hypno-related mimes.

◎ The game
In this activity, participants deliver and decipher mimes of client conditions, within their group. Participants will take turns delivering to the group a mime of a presenting condition. The group has 1 minute to guess what is being mimed before the next person delivers a mime.

Examples include: Nail-biting, performance anxiety, fear of bees, shyness, jealousy, vaping cessation, teeth grinding (bruxism) and stress.

💻 Online adaptations
The activity card can be read to the group by the facilitator. It may also be helpful to post the activity card 'what to do' information in the group chat, for participants to refer to.

👍👍 Development outcome
Knowledge
Participants will gain deeper insight into their knowledge of client conditions by considering how to communicate them non-verbally.

Skills
Participants will experience using their non-verbal observation skills, and also boost their confidence in presenting to a group.

☑ Preparation, resources and props
None.

⧗ Activity card
One activity card is to be given to the group. It is to contain the following information:

Activity
- Timely conditions.

Type of activity
- This is an individual challenge activity.
- You will be using your non-verbal communication skills.

What to do
- In this activity, you will deliver and decipher mimes of client conditions, within your group.
- You will take turns delivering to the group a mime of a presenting condition.
- The group has 1 minute to guess what is being mimed. Then the next person delivers a mime to the group.
- Examples include: Nail-biting, performance anxiety, fear of bees, shyness, jealousy, vaping cessation, teeth grinding (bruxism) and stress.

#60 Tray Memory

📁 Category
Action
Memory
Skill development

📖 Classification
A pairs-within-group, hypnosis activity, for in-person use.

🚩 Overview
Game participants engage in a memory and recall activity using a tray of objects.

◎ The game
This activity which explores the impact of hypnosis on information recall. The group divides into in pairs (or 3s, with third as observer). In the pair one person is rapidly hypnotised and then asked to observe a tray ('hypno tray') for 1 minute. They are then re-alerted and asked to list what they recall. Then they are given another tray ('alert tray') and asked to observe that for 1 minute. When that time has elapsed, they are asked to list what they recall. A comparison can be made, whether there is any difference between how their hypnotic and non-hypnotic memory works. Where possible, some pairs will use the hypno tray, then alert tray, and other pairs will use the alert tray and then hypno tray. Finally, the group can discuss whether there is any impact of hypnosis on memory and information recall.

👍👍 Development outcome
Knowledge
Participants engage in research and gain insight into their own response and how others respond.

Skills
Participants gain experience and develop their research skills.

☑ Preparation, resources and props
Covered trays with contents
You will need to prepare a number of trays, with covers, with 20 random items on the trays e.g., bottle opener, matchbox, toffee, coffee bean and so forth. If you group two pairs together, then they could share trays, as they will only be using one tray at a time.

Record sheet
A record sheet so that participants can note the outcome. This can be simple, such as,

- Date
- Name
- Hypno-tray score
- Alert-tray score

⧗ Activity card
One activity card is to be given to the group. It is to contain the following information:

Activity
- Tray memory.

Type of activity
- This is a pairs hypnosis activity.
- You will be exploring the impact of hypnosis on information recall.

What to do
- In your group, divide into pairs (or 3s, with third as observer).

- Within the pairs, one person takes on the role of hypnotist, and one as research subject.
- The research subject is then rapidly hypnotised by the hypnotist and told to observe a tray ('hypno tray') for 1 minute.
- They are then re-alerted and asked to list what they recall.
- The research subject is then given another tray ('alert tray') and told to observe that for 1 minute.
- When that time has elapsed, they are asked to list what they recall.
- A comparison can then be made, whether there is any difference between how their hypnotic and non-hypnotic memory works.
- Where possible, some pairs will use the hypno tray, then alert tray, and other pairs will use the alert tray and then hypno tray.
- Finally, the group can discuss whether there is any impact of hypnosis on information recall.

Resources
- Two covered trays with contents per pair / trio.
- One record sheet per person.

#61 Triple Promo

📁 Category
Creation
Skill development

📖 Classification
A trio-within-group, talking activity, for online or in-person use.

🚩 Overview
Game participants create hypno promotional strategies.

◎ The game
This activity is focused on creating a hypnotherapy promotional strategy. Within the group, participants divide into groups of three, collaboratively discuss and then create a hypno promo strategy, either online or offline. Where time permits, the group will share their strategy with another group.

💻 Online adaptations
Firstly, the facilitator can invite participants to locate a pen and some paper, or open an online note-taking facility. The activity card can be read to the group by the facilitator. The group can then be assigned, into trios to breakout rooms. It may also be helpful to post the activity card 'what to do' information in the breakout rooms, for participants to refer to. Where time permits, the trios can be brought back into the main room and take turns presenting the strategy to the whole group.

👍 Development outcome
Knowledge
Participants make use of their knowledge of marketing and will gain from the knowledge and ideas of others.

Skills
Participants expand their marketing communication skills.

☑ Preparation, resources and props
Note-taking resources
A flipchart, whiteboard, post-it-notes or even some pens and paper.

⧖ Activity card
One activity card is to be given to the group. It is to contain the following information:

Activity
- Triple promo.

Type of activity
- This is a trio- in-group collaborative talking activity
- You will be using your creativity and knowledge of hypnosis.

What to do
- Within your group, divide into groups of three, collaboratively discuss and then create a hypnotherapy promotional strategy, either online or offline.
- Where time permits, share your strategy with another group.

Resources
- A flipchart, whiteboard, post-it-notes or even some pens and paper.

#62 Tweet Taglines – Hypnotherapy

📁 Categories
Creation
Sharing
Skill development

📖 Classification
A collaborative group activity, for in-person or online use.

🏳 Overview
Game participants create some brief, powerful hypno promotional phrases.

◎ The game
This activity is focused on brief, yet effective communication in the form of promotional phrases. The whole group will work together collaboratively to generate some powerful phrases, that promote hypnotherapy, using 140 characters or less.

💻 Online adaptations
Prior to starting the game, the facilitator can invite participants to locate a pen and paper (or suggest this ahead of time) or open an online note-taking resource. The activity card can then be read to the group by the facilitator. It may also be helpful to post the activity card 'what to do' information in the group chat, for participants to refer to.

👍👍 Development outcome
Knowledge
The activity engages participants' knowledge of hypnosis and marketing, and provides an opportunity to learn from others.

Skills

Participants expand their ability to express themselves effectively, yet briefly. They also gain experience in creating impactful promotional phrases.

☑ Preparation, resources and props

Note-taking
Some pens and paper.

⧖ Activity card

One activity card is to be given to the group. It is to contain the following information:

Activity
- Tweet taglines – hypnotherapy.

Type of activity
- This is a collaborative talking activity for the whole group.
- You will be using your creativity and knowledge of hypnosis.

What to do
- As a group, collaboratively work together to generate some powerful phrases that promote hypnotherapy, whilst only using 140 characters or less.

Resources
- Some pens and paper.

#63 Tweet Taglines – Personal Brand

📁 Categories
Creation
Sharing
Skill development

📖 Classification
An individual-within-group, talking activity.

🚩🚩 Overview
Game participants consider their own personal brands, summarise their brand into a short phrase and then present that to the group.

◎ The game
This activity explores personal brands, with participants each summarising their brand, so that they can be expressed in 140 characters or less. Participants have 5 minutes to create a tweet-style phrase (140 characters or less) that describes their personal brand. They will then present them to the group, and the group will give helpful feedback.

💻 Online adaptations
Prior to starting the game, the facilitator can invite participants to locate a pen and paper (or suggest this ahead of time) or open an online note-taking resource. The activity card can then be read to the group by the facilitator. It may also be helpful to post the activity card 'what to do' information in the group chat, for participants to refer to.

👍👍 Development outcome
Knowledge
The activity engages participants' perspectives of their personal brand and marketing provides an opportunity to get feedback from others.

Skills
Participants expand their ability to express themselves effectively, yet briefly.

☑ Preparation, resources and props
Note-taking
Some pens and paper.

⌛ Activity card
One activity card is to be given to the group. It is to contain the following information:

Activity
- Tweet taglines – personal brand.

Type of activity
- This is an individual talking activity.
- You will be exploring your own personal perspective and that of others.

What to do
- Within your group, individually you will have 5 minutes to create a tweet-style phrase (140 characters or less) that summaries your personal brand.
- You will then take turns to present them to the group, and the group will give you helpful feedback.

Resources
- Some pens and paper.

#64 Two Truths and One Lie

📁 Category
Puzzle
Sharing
Skill development

📖 Classification
An individual-within-group, talking activity, for in-person and online use.

🚩 Overview
Game participants take turns presenting and assessing others telling lies and the truth.

◎ The game
This is an observation skills activity for the whole group. Within your group, each participant takes a turn to tell the group two lies and one truth. The group are to observe the participant's non-verbal communication and work out which of the three statements is true. The group can ask up to two verifying questions for each statement. Individuals can vote (e.g., raised hands) which are the truths and which the lie. Then the next participant gets to offer their three statements.

💻 Online adaptations
The activity card can be read to the group by the facilitator. It may also be helpful to post the activity card 'what to do' information in the group chat, for participants to refer to.

👍👍 Development outcome
Knowledge
Participants apply and refine their existing lie detection knowledge and learn from how others apply theirs.

Skills
This activity engages participants' listening and observational skills.

☑ Preparation, resources and props
None required.

⧗ Activity card
One activity card is to be given to the group. It is to contain the following information:

Activity
- Two truths and one lie.

Type of activity
- This is an individual challenge talking activity.
- You will be using your communication skills.

What to do
- In this observation skills game, within your group, each participant takes a turn to tell the group two lies and one truth.
- The group observe the participant's non-verbal communication and work out which of the three statements is true.
- As a group, you can ask up to two verifying questions for each statement.
- Within the group, individuals can vote (e.g., raised hands) which are the truths and which the lie.
- Then, the next participant gets to offer their three statements.

#65 Vocab Variety – Anxiety

📁 Category
Cognitive challenge
Sharing
Sport

📖 Classification
An individual-within-group, competitive talking activity, for in-person or online use.

⚑ Overview
Game participants offer alternative words for common anxiety terms.

◎ The game
In this whole group activity, participants explore other names for common anxiety terms. The group will sit in a circle. Starting with one person, they will go around the circle, with each person giving one alternative name for the first topic. If they cannot give a name within 5 seconds, they drop out of that round. The winner is the last one remaining and they get to start the next round.

Topics: Anxiety, Stress, Fear, Worry, Panic.

💻 Online adaptations
The activity card can be read to the group by the facilitator. It may also be helpful to post the activity card 'what to do' information in the group chat, for participants to refer to.

👍👍 Development outcome
Knowledge
Participants engage their knowledge of hypnosis-related language and

learn from the terms that others use.

Skills
Participants use their linguistic and communication skills.

☑ Preparation, resources and props
None required

⌛ Activity card
One activity card is to be given to the group. It is to contain the following information:

Activity
- Vocab variety – anxiety.

Type of activity
- This is an individual competitive talking activity.
- You will be using your language skills.

What to do
- In this whole group activity, you will be exploring other names for common anxiety terms. The group is to sit in a circle.
- Starting with one person, they will go around the circle with each person giving one alternative name for the first topic.
- If they don't' give a name within 5 seconds, they drop out of that round.
- The winner is the last one remaining and they get to start the next round.
- Topics: Anxiety, Stress, Fear, Worry, Panic.

#66 Vocab Variety – Hypno

📁 Category
Cognitive challenge
Sharing
Sport

📖 Classification
An individual-within-group, competitive talking activity, for in-person and online use.

🚩 Overview
Game participants offer alternative words for common hypno terms.

🎯 The game
In this whole group activity, participants explore other names for common hypno terms. The group will sit in a circle. Starting with one person, they will go around the circle, with each person giving one alternative name for the first topic. If they cannot give a name within 5 seconds, they drop out of that round. The winner is the last one remaining and they get to start the next round.

Theme topics: Suggestibility test, induction, deepener, awakening, hypnotherapy, hypnotherapist.

💻 Online adaptations
The activity card can be read to the group by the facilitator. It may also be helpful to post the activity card 'what to do' information in the group chat, for participants to refer to.

👐 Development outcome

Knowledge
Participants engage their knowledge of hypnosis-related language and learn from the terms that others use.

Skills
Participants use their linguistic and communication skills.

☑ Preparation, resources and props
None required

⌛ Activity card
One activity card is to be given to the group. It is to contain the following information:

Activity
- Vocab variety – hypno.

Type of activity
- This is an individual competitive talking activity.
- You will be using your language skills.

What to do
- In this whole group activity, you will be exploring other names for common anxiety terms. The group is to sit in a circle.
- Starting with one person, they will go around the circle, with each person giving one alternative name for the first topic.
- If they cannot give a name within 5 seconds, they drop out of that round.
- The winner is the last one remaining and they get to start the next round.
- Theme topics: Suggestibility test, induction, deepener, awakening, hypnotherapy, hypnotherapist.

#67 Vocab Variety – Recreational Drugs

📁 Category
Cognitive challenge
Sharing
Skill development
Sport

📖 Classification
Individual within group, competitive talking activity, for in-person and online use.

🏳 Overview
Game participants will offer alternative words for common recreational drug terms.

◎ The game
In this whole group activity, participants explore other names for common recreational drug words and terms. The group will sit in a circle. Starting with one person, they will go around the circle, with each person giving one alternative name for the first topic. If they cannot give a name within 5 seconds, they drop out of that round. The winner is the last one remaining and they get to start the next round.

Theme topics: Cocaine, Cannabis, Heroin, Ecstasy, Ketamine, Intoxicated.

💻 Online adaptations
The activity card can be read to the group by the facilitator. It may also be helpful to post the activity card 'what to do' information in the group chat, for participants to refer to.

👍👍 Development outcome

Knowledge
Participants engage their knowledge of hypnosis-related and drug-related language and learn from the terms that others use.

Skills
Participants use their linguistic and communication skills.

☑ Preparation, resources and props
None required.

⏳ Activity card
One activity card is to be given to the group. It is to contain the following information:

Activity
- Vocab variety – recreational drugs.

Type of activity
- This is an individual competitive talking activity.
- You will be using your language skills.

What to do
- In this whole group activity, you will be exploring other names for common recreational drug terms. The group is to sit in a circle.
- Starting with one person, they will go around the circle, with each person giving one alternative name for the first topic.
- If they cannot give a name within 5 seconds, they drop out of that round.
- The winner is the last one remaining and they get to start the next round.
- Theme topics: Cocaine, Cannabis, Heroin, Ecstasy, Ketamine

#68 Vocab Variety – Sexual Words

📁 Category
Comfort-zone expansion
Cognitive challenge
Sharing
Sport

📖 Classification
An individual-within-group, competitive talking activity, for in-person and online use.

🚩 Overview
Game participants offer alternative words for common sexual words and terms.

◎ The game
In this whole group activity, participants explore other names for common sexual words and terms. The participant group will sit in a circle. Starting with one person, they will go around the circle, with each person giving one alternative name for the first topic. If they cannot give a name within 5 seconds, they drop out of that round. The winner is the last one remaining and they get to start the next round.

Theme topics: Penis, Vagina, Breasts, Sex

💻 Online adaptations
The activity card can be read to the group by the facilitator. It may also be helpful to post the 'what to do' information in the group chat, for participants to refer to.

Development outcome
Knowledge
Participants engage their knowledge of sexual and hypnosis-related language and learn from the terms that others use.

Skills
Participants use their linguistic and communication skills.

☑ Preparation, resources and props
None required.

⧖ Activity card
One activity card is to be given to the group. It is to contain the following information:

Activity
- Vocab variety – sexual words.

Type of activity
- This is an individual competitive talking activity.
- You will be using your language skills.

What to do
- In this whole group activity, you will be exploring other names for common sexual words and terms. The group is to sit in a circle.
- Starting with one person, they will go around the circle, with each person giving one alternative name for the first topic.
- If they cannot give a name within 5 seconds, they drop out of that round.
- The winner is the last one remaining and they get to start the next round.
- Theme topics: Penis, Vagina, Breasts, Sex

#69 Vocation Variety – Group Induction

📁 Category
Role-playing
Skill development

📖 Classification
A group challenge experience, with hypnosis, for in-person and online use.

🚩 Overview
Game participants take turns adopting a persona and delivering a hypnosis experience as that person. The group then attempts to identify the persona portrayed.

◎ The game
Within the group, one person takes on the persona of a famous hypno-related figure and delivers, to the group, a short hypnosis experience, as though they were that person. The group, once re-alerted, then discuss the persona in an effort to identify who that figure is. If time permits, another person can then take a turn, but with a different persona.

💻 Online adaptations
The activity card can be read to the group by the facilitator. It may also be helpful to post the activity card 'what to do' information in the group chat, for participants to refer to.

👍👍 Development outcome
Knowledge
This activity requires the participants to connect to their knowledge of hypno-related figures.

Skills

For the hypnotist, there are opportunities to develop their role-playing, vocal flexibility and group hypnosis skills. For the group participants, they will be able to engage their observation skills.

☑ Preparation, resources and props

None required.

⌛ Activity card

One activity card is to be given to the group. It is to contain the following information:

Activity
- Vocation variety – group induction.

Type of activity
- This is a hypnosis challenge activity for the group.
- You will be using your hypnosis knowledge and skills.

What to do
- Within the group, one person takes on the persona of a famous hypno-related figure and delivers a short hypnosis experience to the group, as though they were that person.
- The group, once re-alerted then discuss the persona in an effort to identify who that figure is.
- If time permits, another person can then take a turn, but with a different persona.

#70 What Would You Do If?

📁 Category
Dilemma

Sharing

📖 Classification
A group talking activity, for in-person and online use.

🚩 Overview
Game participants discuss their response to specified hypno-related scenarios.

◎ The game
In this activity, the group discusses several potential client scenarios and the possible responses to a range of situations. The group will start with the first topic, for 2 minutes and then move on to the next.

💻 Online adaptations
The activity card can be read to the group by the facilitator. It may also be helpful to post the activity card 'what to do' information in the group chat, for participants to refer to, as well as the information from the scenarios card.

👍👍 Development outcome
Knowledge
Participants explore their own views, perceptions and biases and those of others.

Skills
Participants use and develop their communication skills.

☑ Preparation, resources and props
Scenarios card
Print the following scenarios, either on one card or individual cards.

1. Your client walks in and says coffee, skimmed milk and three sugars please.
2. Your client had booked a session to stop nail biting, but, when they arrive, they say that they want a session on improving their orgasms.
3. A client sends you a large cash tip with a note asking you to burn their client records.
4. A male client sends you an explicit photo of himself, naked, and asks how hypnotherapy can help him.
5. A client asks if you will spend a long-weekend with them, on their yacht, in case they are in need of your services. You have been working with them on weight management (weight loss) issues.

⧗ Activity card
One activity card is to be given to the group. It is to contain the following information:

Activity
- What would you do if?

Type of activity
- This is a collaborative group discussion activity.
- You will be exploring several scenarios.

What to do
- In this activity, your group will discuss several potential client scenarios and the possible responses to a range of situations. Start with the first topic, for 2 minutes and then move on to the next.

Resources
- Scenarios card.

All Participants Activities

These five games are designed to be used with all of your participants, although there can be teams within the overall group.

Hypno pantomime
This is a creative and collaborative challenge which can be of relatively short, or longer duration. Some breakout space would be useful in the creation phase. An assigned space where the pantomime can be performed and other participants can be seated and watch is useful.

Hypno scavenger hunt
This will benefit from having space in the hypno games location, such as other parts of the building, so that the group can have a more abundant experience.

Magical chairs
Where time is short, this can be a relatively quick game, or it can be made more substantial by adding in other tasks. There needs to be sufficient space and chairs for half of the participants to be seated.

Relay race
This needs sufficient space for a race. For example, 20 metres or more between the start and finish line, plus room for the teams to be in a queue (line) at the start.

Totally trivia
This can be delivered with the participants seated in groups, with a little space between groups.

#71 Hypno Panto

📁 Category
Comfort-zone expansion
Creative
Role-playing

📖 Classification
A collaborative-teams, talking activity, for in-person use.

🏳

Game participants, in teams, create and then deliver hypno-themed pantomimes.

◎ The game
The participants will be divided into large teams and each group will create a short (approx. 5-10 minute) hypno-themed version of any pantomime. Time is allocated for the design of the pantomime, and then each team takes turns to deliver their pantomime to the audience (other teams).

👍👍 Development outcome
Knowledge
Participants draw on their knowledge of hypnosis to create a pantomime with a hypnosis-related theme.

Skills
Participants expand their comfort zone, employing creativity and role-playing skills.

☑ Preparation, resources and props
Space
There needs to be sufficient space for breakout groups and then for the pantomimes to be delivered.

Note-making
Pens and paper will aid planning.

Briefing info
Copies of the briefing sheet for each team.

⌛ Briefing sheet wording
The briefing sheet is issued to each team.

Activity
- Hypno panto.

Type of activity
- This is a large team talking activity.
- You will be engaging your creative skills and using your hypnosis knowledge.

What to do
- Within your allocated team create a short (approx. 5-10 minute) hypno-themed version of any pantomime.
- You will be told how long is allocated for this creative stage.
- Then, each team will take their turn to deliver their panto to the audience (other teams) and you will get to watch the presentations of the other teams.

Resources
- Pens and paper for planning.
- Copies of the briefing sheet for each team.

#72 Hypno Scavenger Hunt: Team -v- Team Version

📁 Category
Action-adventure
Cognitive challenge
Puzzle
Sport

📖 Classification
A collaborative team -v- team, competitive talking activity, for in-person use.

🚩 Overview
Game participants, in teams, have a scavenger hunt.

◎ The game
This is a collaborative group experience, working together to find items. The participants are divided into medium or large teams. Each team is given a list of named items, or a list of clues, relating to things to find. When they find something, they are to note the number on the item and leave it in place. The aim is to find everything and have a full list of item numbers, which can be checked against a master sheet.

👍👍 Development outcome
Knowledge
Participants will use their knowledge of hypnosis and hypnotherapy, together with the experience of working within a team.

Skills
This is great for boosting participants' observation skills and also encourages participants to work collaboratively with people they may not

know, or know well.

☑ Preparation, resources and props
Briefing info
Each team will also benefit from a copy of the briefing sheet.

Photos
Get photos of hypnotic figures and hypnosis-related items (e.g., books, leaflets), label with random numbers (e.g., A4, K3) and hide them 'in plain sight' around the venue (get venue management permission first, if relevant). Remember to collect the items again at the end.

Master number and location list
Also, create a master list of items and their numbers (and locations).

⌛ Briefing sheet wording
The briefing sheet is issued to each team.

Activity
- Hypno scavenger hunt: team – v – team.

Type of activity
- This is a team-v-team collaborative team experience, with each team working together to find items.
- The location boundaries are …. *(Define location boundaries, where they can and cannot go).*

What to do
- Your team will be given a list of named items, or a list of clues, relating to things to find.
- When you find something, you are to note the reference number on the item and leave it in place.
- The aim is to find everything and have a full list of item numbers, which can be checked against a master sheet.

Resources
- You will need the list of items or clues to get started.

#73 Magical Chairs

📁 Category
Action
Skill development
Time challenge

📖 Classification
An individual-within-team, hypnosis activity, for in-person use.

🚩 Overview
Game participants engage in a range of hypno challenges.

◎ The game
This is an individual-within-team, or individual-within-entire-group experience. For a small body of participants (e.g., up to 30) this activity can be run with all participants. For a larger group, the participants can be divided into separate group locations to optimise available space. Chairs are positioned side by side, back-to-back for half of the participants. Half of the group (e.g., 10) are seated, the other half (e.g., 10) stand, one in front of each seated person.

Those standing deliver the first challenge. Then those standing move along one place to the next seated person and deliver the next challenge. When all of the challenges have been achieved, those seated stand and those standing become seated (i.e., they swap places), and the challenges are repeated. A facilitator will call out the challenges and monitor times (where relevant).

👍👍 Development outcome
Knowledge
Participants are able to engage with their knowledge of hypnotic topics, tests and inductions, and learn from watching and experiencing others.

Skills
Participants are able to engage with existing skills in a new way.

☑ Preparation, resources and props
List
A list of challenges for the facilitator.

Space and chairs
Sufficient space to set out the chairs of a suitable type (e.g., avoid folding or flimsy).

⧖ Briefing sheet wording
The briefing sheet is issued to the facilitator.

Activity
- Magical chairs.

Type of activity
- This is an individual within a team or group hypnosis activity.
- You will engage in a range of hypnosis-related tasks.

What to do
- This is an individual within a team (or entire group) experience.
- A facilitator will call out the challenges and monitor times (where relevant).
- For a small body of participants (e.g., up to 40) this activity can be run with all participants. For a larger group, the participants can be divided into separate group locations to optimise available space.
- Chairs are positioned side by side, back-to-back for half of the participants, thus a row of 10 chairs, side by side, with another row, mirroring this, chair back to chair back. Half of the group (e.g., 20) are to be seated, the other half (e.g., 20) stand, one in front of each seated person.

- Those standing deliver the first challenge. Then those standing move along one place to the next seated person and deliver the next challenge. When all challenges have been achieved, those seated stand and those standing become seated (i.e., they swap places), and the challenges are repeated.
- Examples of challenges are,

    1. Movement-based suggestibility test
    2. Catalepsy-based suggestibility test
    3. Turn a suggestibility test into an induction
    4. Magnetic something (other than hands/fingers) induction
    5. Physical deepener
    6. Silent mime induction
    7. Confusion induction
    8. Physical induction
    9. 30-second pre-talk
    10. What a hypnotherapist is (30 seconds)

#74 Relay Race

🗁 Category
Comfort-zone expansion
Cognitive challenge
Sharing
Sport

📖 Classification
A team-v-team, competitive talking activity, for in-person use.

🎴 Overview
Game participants, in teams, engage in a hypno-themed relay race.

◎ The game
This is a knowledge-based, race activity. In this game there is a starting point and a target point. At the target point, there will be a chair or table with a box (or similar storage) containing category and answer cards). There will be a checker (assigned person) at each target point. The participants are divided into equal-sized teams. If there are uneven numbers of team participants, assign people to go twice.

The teams stand one behind each other at the starting point. The first person in each team travels to the target point using their assigned method of travel. They find a category card and look through the other cards to find the correct answer card. They present the pair to the checker.

- If correct, the person races back to their team.
- If incorrect, they search until they find a correct answer. The checker keeps the correct cards.

When the first person returns, the next person travels to the target point using the next assigned method of travel. The first team to pair all their categories and answers and return to the starting point is the winning team.

👍👍 Development outcome
Knowledge
Participants will use their general hypnotic knowledge to engage in the relay race.

Skills
Participants will gain experience working as part of a team.

☑ Preparation, resources and props
Briefing info
Print several copies of the briefing sheet – one per team.

Category and answer cards
Print the categories onto cards of one colour (e.g., pink) and the answers on white card. Alternatively, to make the task more challenging, make the cards all the same colour.

For each team, use all the categories and one answer card per category. The teams do not need the same answers. For example, Team A's answer pair for hypnotic phenomena is amnesia and Team B's answer pair for the same category is regression. It is also desirable to include some 'red herring' answers.

Category 1: Hypnotic Phenomena
Dissociation
Catalepsy
Amnesia
Regression
Revivification
Analgesia

Anaesthesia
Hallucinations
Catalepsy
Hypermnesia

Category 2: Historical figures who have contributed to hypno
James Braid
Hippolyte Bernheim
Dave Elman
Sigmund Freud
Milton H. Erickson

Category 3: Indirect Language Pattern
Perhaps you may...
Imagine what it would be like if...
You might...
You could...
You can...
Some people...
Could you...

Category 4: Objective (visible) signs of 'trance'
Glazed eyes
REM or eyelid flicker
Slow deep breathing
Muscle relaxation
Slow physical movements
Following suggestions
Glazed expression
Slumping

Category 5: Suggestibility test
Bucket and balloon (heavy and light hands)
Magnetic fingers

The Lemon
Eye lock
Steel arm
Hand-lock
Magnetic hands
Chevreul's pendulum
Postural sway

Category 6: Types of hypnotic induction
Shock
Permissive
Rapid
Physical relaxation
Direct suggestion
Indirect suggestion
Utilisation

Category 7: Subjective experiences of 'trance' (experienced by person in hypnosis)
Floating or drifting
Heaviness or lightness
Catalepsy
Peaceful
Relaxed
Focus
Time distortion

Category 8: Components of a hypnotherapy session
Pre-talk
Client consultation
Scaling
Goals
Treatment plan discussion
Consent
Hypnotic state generation (induction deepener)

Suggestibility test
Suggestions
Therapy technique
Awakening
Homework

Category 9: Red herrings (don't print as category)
Green
Purple
Blue
Wrist
Waist
Doorway
Unicorn
Counselling
Rigidity
Floppiness
Dreaming

⌛ Briefing sheet wording
One copy of the briefing sheet is to be issued to each team.

Activity
- Relay race.

Type of activity
- This is a team-v-team competitive talking activity.
- You will be using your hypnosis knowledge.

What to do
- In this game there is a starting point and a target point.
- At the target point, there will be a chair or table with a box (or similar storage) containing category and answer cards).
- There will be a checker (assigned person) at each target point.

- You will have been divided into teams. The teams stand one behind each other at the starting point.
- The first person in each team travels to the target point using their assigned method of travel.
- They find a category card and look through the other cards to find the correct answer card.
- They present the pair to the checker.
    - If correct, the person races back to their team.
    - If incorrect, they search until they find a correct answer. The checker keeps the correctly-paired cards.
- When the first person returns, the next person travels to the target point using the next assigned method of travel.
- The first team to pair all their categories and answers and return to the starting point is the winning team.

Assigned methods of travel
1. Forwards
2. Sideways
3. Backwards
4. Skip
5. Clap
6. Circles
7. Flap arms
8. Three people making a circle around the assigned person

#75 Totally Trivia

📁 Category
Cognitive challenge
Quiz
Sport

📖 Classification
A collaborative, team-v-team, competitive talking activity for in-person or online use.
OR
An individual-within-group, competitive talking activity for online use (adapt game accordingly).

📌 Overview
Game participants, whether in teams or as individuals, answer hypno-related trivia questions.

◎ The game
This is a team activity within the entire group. Participants form into teams of 5-8 people. They will have one answer sheet per team. A quiz master (facilitator) will call out a number of questions. Each team agrees an answer and writes it down. The winning team has the highest number of correct answers.

💻 Online adaptations
The activity card can be read to the group by the facilitator. The questions can be read to an entire group and participants can work individually to answer the questions. Alternatively, the facilitator can move participants, as teams, into breakout rooms and post the questions, one at a time, (or together) in the breakout room chat. Another option is to use a survey tool, such as survey monkey, and give participants access to a link to the online quiz, which, depending on how it is set up, could also auto-mark

the submissions.

👍👍 Development outcome

Knowledge
Participants will use their general hypnotic knowledge to contribute within their team and also learn from the answers of other team-mates.

Skills
Participants will gain experience working collaboratively as part of a team.

☑ Preparation, resources and props

Answer sheet
A blank answer sheet (page with numbers and space to write brief answers) to be given to each team.

Trivia questions (with answers)
One line of questions, with the answers, to be given to the facilitator.

Sample trivia questions (answers in brackets)
1. What is Mesmer's full name?
   (Franz Anton Mesmer)
2. What nationality was James Braid?
   (Scottish)
3. What was hypnotist Bernheim's first name?
   (Hippolyte)
4. Where did Sigmund Freud study hypnotism?
   (Paris School – could accept Nancy School as briefly visited there)
5. What is the name of Dave Elman's book which commonly has a green cover?
   (Hypnotherapy)
6. What is Milton Erickson's middle name?
   (Hyland)

7. *Which hypnosis society had Milton Erickson as the founding president?*
   (American Society for Clinical Hypnosis)
8. *A widely used hypnosis research tool has the abbreviation SHSS. What does this represent?*
   (Stanford Hypnotic Susceptibility Scale)
9. *What is the name of the UK legislation relating to hypnosis?*
   (The Hypnotism Act 1952)
10. *What is the name of the movie, involving hypnosis, about three company workers who hate their jobs and decide to rebel against the greedy boss, with Jennifer Aniston?*
    (Office Space)
11. *The Arons Scale of Hypnotic Depth has how many stages?*
    (Six)
12. *Who is associated with the phrase 'Day by day, in every way, I am getting better and better'?*
    (Emil Coue)
13. *Which doctor worked in Calcutta in 1845 and performed surgery with the patient's pain being addressed by hypnosis?* (James Esdaile)
14. *In which country were there 'sleep temples'?*
    (Greece)
15. *In the Hypnotic Induction Profile, what happens to a person's eyes to indicate they are fully hypnotised?*
    (Roll up/backwards)
16. *What is the name of the movie with an art auctioneer, a group of criminals, a hypnotherapist and a painting?*
    (Trance)
17. *Which physician is associated with the term 'animal magnetism'?*
    (Franz Anton Mesmer)
18. *What is the name of the 1894 book, written by George du Maurier, with the character Svengali?*
    (Trilby)
19. *What language does the word 'Hypnos' come from?*
    (Ancient Greek)

20. *In what year did the British Medical Association recognise hypnosis as a beneficial therapeutic tool?*
(1955)

⏳ Briefing / answer sheet wording
Activity
- Totally trivia.

Type of activity
- This is a team-v-team talking activity.
- You will be using your hypnosis knowledge.

What to do
- In your team you will make note of the answers to the questions that a quiz master (facilitator) will call out.
- Within your team agree an answer and write it down.
- The winning team has the highest number of correct answers.

Additional Products and Services

For more information, please visit:

DrKateHypno.com

The PADLE Corporate Communications Consultancy

How much more successful could you or your organisation be with better developed, more effective communication approaches?

The PADLE corporate communication system is a highly interactive programme offering a blend of strategies using presentations, illustrated with real-life scenarios, together with practical activities designed to rapidly develop communication skills, confidence and competence.

Participants will discover key factors of effective communication, understand what it means to be a good communicator and learn how to engage and influence their audience, large or small, in any situation. The PADLE corporate communication system consists of five phases which are customised to suit organisational requirements.

Phase 1
A detailed assessment of internal and external communications and corporate core values, together with needs analysis, training plans and outcome assessment processes.

Phase 2
Individual, team or corporate-wide training, to enhance and maximise spoken and written communication effectiveness in a wide range of

situations and environments.

Phase 3

Targeted, bespoke and individual training for positive professional performance, considering personal and professional self-talk, together with enhanced interpersonal communication.

Phase 4

Persuasive leadership communication skills for directing positive behaviour, perceptions and culture from ground-floor to board-level.

Phase 5

Advanced language shaping skills to develop communication confidence and competence in a wide range of scenarios.

Full details can be found on DrKateHypno.com

1-to-1 Presentation Skills Consultancy

Would you like to maximise your communication effectiveness? Give exciting and interesting presentations that hold your audience's attention and interest? These are skills which, once learned and practiced, will support you for a lifetime.

Good presentation skills can help you climb the career ladder and have applications far wider than you might think. Confidence, self-assurance and poise, developed with your presentations, can shine through naturally in all aspects of your life whether effectively presenting your case to a management or executive board, asking for a pay rise, addressing a large conference, or throughout your leisure and personal life.

Whether you want to get rid of performance nerves and anxiety, or brush up on your stage craft, this detailed and highly interactive consultancy program will help you develop new skills and enhance current abilities. You will be able to develop an understanding of what makes an effective presentation and how to avoid the potential pitfalls.

Individual coaching sessions start with a thorough assessment of your presentation skills and needs and then continues with a tailored, yet comprehensive program, which addresses the entire presentation event(s), from the initial invitation or application, through to preparation, the actual presentation and maximising the benefits during the post-presentation stage.

Dr Kate has extensive experience at presenting in a wide range of environments, include large audiences at conferences (1,000+ delegates) and enjoys sharing that experience, teaching people from a broad range of industries how to excel at presenting. Full details can be found on .www.DrKateHypno.com

Speaking Engagements

I truly enjoy giving presentations and demonstrations, and I am available to speak at a wide range of conferences, dinners, workshops and other events. Some of my presentation topics include:

- Hypnosis (theory, practice, entertainment).
- Hypno-EMDR
- Hypnotherapy (theory, practice, therapy, sport, clinical, case studies).
- Hypnosis and hypnotherapy research.
- Psychology influences on hypnotherapy.
- Personal and professional communication.
- The psychology of language in the workplace.
- Personal and professional development.
- Presentation skills and tips.
- Research methods and skills.
- Teaching hypnotherapy.
- Use games to enhance learning and development.

To enquire about booking me as a speaker for your event, please contact me at **www.DrKateHypno.com**

1-to-1 Presenter Coaching and Mentoring

Superb presentation skills can help you increase your profile and develop your business. Yet the benefits of excellent presentation skills reach far wider than you might think.

Confidence, self-assurance and poise, developed with your presentations, can shine through naturally in all aspects of your life, whether effectively presenting your case to a management or executive board, asking for a pay rise, addressing a large conference, or throughout your leisure and personal life.

Whether you want to get rid of performance nerves and anxiety, or brush up on your stage craft, this detailed and highly interactive coaching programme will help you develop new skills and enhance current abilities.

You will be able to develop an understanding of what makes an effective presentation and how to avoid the potential pitfalls. I have extensive experience at presenting in a wide range of environments, including large audiences at conferences (1,000+ delegates) and enjoy sharing that experience, teaching people how to excel at giving powerful presentations and memorable demonstrations.

1-to-1 coaching

Individual coaching sessions start with a thorough assessment of your presentation skills and needs, and then continue with a tailored, yet comprehensive programme, which addresses the entire presentation event(s), from the initial invitation or application, through preparation, to the actual presentation and maximising the benefits during the post-presentation stage.

You can book either a half day (4 hours) or a full day (8 hours) where we will explore your individual needs and intensively cover anything you need to develop more skill and confidence, whether in your presentations or hypnosis demonstrations. There will be lots of practice and constructive feedback.

Strategic mentoring

I also offer shorter mentoring sessions for those hypnotists who're already giving presentations/demonstrations and are looking to refine specific aspects of their skills. Mentoring sessions can be held via Skype/Zoom or over the phone and can be booked in 15-minute chunks as required.

To find out more about presenter coaching and mentoring, please contact me directly via **www.drkatehypno.com**

Hypnosis and Hypnotherapy Training

An enthusiastic and positive teacher, passionate about great training, I teach clinical and non-clinical students a broad range of hypnosis and hypnotherapy theory and practice all over the world. I have extensive teaching experience, including within organisations, as well as both higher education (Universities) and further education (Colleges), on topics including hypnotherapy, psychology, research methods and study skills.

My teaching practice has been formally assessed and has received two 'Outstanding' ratings. I am a Certified Instructor for the National Guild of Hypnotists and am both a Fellow of the Higher Education Academy (Advance HE) and Fellow of the Society for Education and Training.

1-to-1 bespoke training

I provide bespoke 1-to-1 training on hypnosis and hypnotherapy theory and practice. Whether you are a complete novice, seeking some general refresher training, or are looking for focused and highly individual training at a specialist, or advanced practitioner level, I can deliver the specific training you need.

If you are unsure of what you need, I will work with you to conduct a knowledge and skills analysis, prior to formulating your training plan. For medics, those in all areas of healthcare, emergency responders and the military, I also provide customised 1-to-1 fast-track hypnotherapy training.

Training can be broad, covering the scope of hypnotherapy practitioner training, or focused around specific topics, such as trauma, pain management, anxiety, mental toughness and resilience and conversational (alert) hypnosis techniques. Full details can be found on www.DrKateHypno.com

Live practitioner training

I am lead trainer and founder of award-winning HypnoTC: The Hypnotherapy Training Company. The HypnoTC Professional Hypnotherapy Diploma is one of the most comprehensive and practical hypnotherapy courses available in the UK today, and frequently has students flying in from international locations solely to participate in the course.

Teaching is provided in a supportive classroom environment. Each tuition day will include theoretical lectures, presentations and discussions, together with practical demonstrations, group activities and practice of techniques taught. The course notes are supplemented by additional online materials, according to the topics being covered. Full details can be found on www.HypnoTC.com

Online training

As well as all of the live training options, I also have a vast range of online hypnosis and hypnotherapy training courses. For those looking for an effective introduction to hypnotherapy, the **'Hypnotherapy 101'** course, which consists of over 6.5 hours intensive video training as well as a comprehensive 150-page course manual may be ideal. For those with more knowledge or specific needs, there are courses on topics such as becoming a confident hypnotist, goal setting, metaphors, rapid therapy approaches and pain management for hypnotherapists. So, if you'd like to check out our range of online courses (which is always

being added to), you can get immediate access right now, here
www.Hypnosis-Courses.com

Books

How to Communicate More Effectively

This book offers insight into how we communicate, both with others and with ourselves, showing you how to engage with a range of 'real-world' spoken and non-verbal strategies and personal skills, to elevate the effectiveness of your communication beyond just simple words.

By gaining a better understanding of how to communicate more effectively, you will quickly learn how language can positively influence all aspects of your life.

Whether you want to learn to positively influence others in your workplace, or enjoy better relationships with friends or family, this book will give you the tools to transform both your communication skills and the way you think about yourself as a communicator.

Powerful Hypnosis Presentations:
The HypnoDemo® Approach

Great presentations and awesome demonstrations showcase how great you are at what you do, promoting yourself as the expert and boosting your professional profile.

This book will help you to understand all the key elements that can help you deliver highly effective presentations to stimulate interest in your hypnosis skills, sell your services, and make you memorable to potential clients.

By developing the knowledge and skills to give great presentations and fantastic demonstrations, you can even start to enjoy them!

You will find that this book follows the HypnoDemo ® approach, addressing the key aspects of giving an effective presentation, including how to perform a great hypnosis demonstration. It will help you develop all aspects of your presentation, from initial concept through to gaining insight and learning afterwards.

You will discover how to enhance and add impact to your presentations and demonstrations, increase your professional confidence, and enable yourself to enjoy the entire process.

Sam the Sleepy Sheep

This innovative new book has been specifically designed to help put children to sleep.

Written using the combined expertise of two hypnotherapy experts, myself and Rory Z. Fulcher, the book uses sleep-inducing hypnotic language patterns, which easily and effectively get children to close their eyes and go to sleep.

This book takes bed-time communication to a new level.

Full details of all my books can be found on Amazon (worldwide) as well as on **www.DrKateHypno.com**

Cards

Hypnotic language cards

These are a great way to learn and integrate indirect (or Ericksonian) language patterns into your own communications. The language patterns presented in these cards are ideal for adding an edge to your presentations and enhancing your storytelling, as well as contributing to your effectiveness in hypnosis, NLP and coaching sessions. In fact, helping you to communicate well and increase your ability to subtly influence people in your normal daily interactions.

When you buy these cards, you automatically get free access to the online instruction guide that shows you exactly how to best use these cards effectively and to integrate the knowledge both consciously and subconsciously for ease of use. Full details can be found on **www.DrKateHypno.com**

Core values cards

These core values cards can be used by therapists and coaches to discover their client's core values, as well as by individuals interested in personal and professional development. An awareness of a person's core values is an integral contribution towards a successful goal-setting process and will increase the likelihood of success when working to achieve goals.

These cards come with comprehensive instructions for use (webpage) and are an invaluable personal development tool. Full details can be found on **www.DrKateHypno.com**

Thank you for reading!

I hope that you have enjoyed reading this Hypno Games book and have found some interesting and useful ways of gaining learning and development whilst having fun!

I would totally appreciate you taking the time to leave a quick review of this Hypno Games book on Amazon. It helps others to make the right choice, knowing they are able to buy with confidence. Your experience of this book offers a powerful guide for what others can expect. I do read each review myself and really enjoy reading your comments, thoughts and experiences of using the games in this book. So, feel free to be honest in your review.

If you have any questions or comments (especially on how you have used the games in this book), or you would like me to work with you or your organisation, or run the games at an event, do please contact me personally via my website **www.DrKateHypno.com**

Dr Kate Beaven-Marks